Tenacious

Tenacious

One Man's Lifelong Struggle for Justice

George Washington Hall

With L. R. Turochy

Published by The Fifty Fund

Published in the United States of America by The Fifty Fund, Auburn, Alabama.

ISBN: 979-8-9875197-0-7
LCCN: 2023904923

This book is George Washington Hall's memoir. It reflects his present recollections of experiences over time.

All photographs used with permission from the George Washington Hall Collection at the Alabama Department of Archives and History.

Book cover design by Elizabeth Turochy.

Acknowledgments

Mary Reynolds McInnis and Robert Raymond

I would not have done it without you.

- G.W.H.

Contents

Foreword

A century ago, more than 100,000 Black farmers tilled the rich soils of Alabama. By 2017, according to the U.S. Department of Agriculture census, there were barely 4,000.

George Washington Hall has been among their dwindling numbers for nearly three-quarters of the past century, steadfastly working his family's land in Greene County, Alabama from the time he first picked vegetables and cotton at the side of his grandmother. In conversations with him over the years, particularly in recent ones, George has lamented the increasingly lonely status of the Black farmer, worrying what it meant not only for the deteriorating social and geographic fabric of Alabama's Black Belt but also for the declining health, wealth, and food security of all those communities. Without the farmers, who is growing the food that fills the farmers markets and nourishes the neighborhood? Who is bringing life not only to the soil but to the countryside, to the rural heartland of this country?

George worried about all of that. "We're almost extinct," he would say.

Thank goodness, then, that George has favored us with his story, **this** story which you now hold in your hands. So that we will always remember, and, as George fervently hopes, may one day bring forth a revival.

This book is a treasure on several fronts. It is the story of a farmer, and as such it is a chronicle of soil and seeds, of fertilizer and finance, of hope at the planting and despair at the droughts (and floods, and winds, and pests, and turbulent economics), of joy over the harvests and the sharing of food with neighbors and a nation. It is also the story of a Black farmer in Alabama, and thus it is a story of racism and discrimination, of protests and arrests, of poverty and perseverance, of resistance and resilience. And, above all, this is a story of America, and so it is a tale of dreaming big and working hard, of public service and patriotism, of the resolute struggle for liberty, justice and equal treatment under the law, and of an abiding faith – despite being tested again and again -- that truth and righteousness will prevail.

With courageous detail, George's memoir takes its rightful place among the hallowed stories of civil rights activists and freedom fighters who have honored this state and this country through the years. And with anecdotes, George's book now, too, resides in the luscious realm of Southern storytelling, soulfully describing an iconic way and place of life.

I was a reporter with *The Wall Street Journal* when I first met George in the 1990s, when his outrage over the blatant discrimination he and fellow Black farmers had experienced propelled him all the way from his farm in Greene County to the halls of power in Washington DC. He and several other farmers – the lead plaintiffs in a massive discrimination suit against the USDA – would pile into one car, clutching sandwiches in paper bags, and drive across the South to the nation's capital with their grievances. On one trip, they arrived at the White House and gave President Clinton and his advisors an earful on right and wrong and their unfair, unjust treatment as Black farmers in America.

George had served his country in Vietnam, fighting for democracy and all it stood for – freedom, equality, justice – only to be denied those same cherished principles upon returning to his farm. He became county sheriff, devoted to upholding equal treatment under the law, while being told at the same time that equal treatment didn't apply to him; the county lending agency repeatedly denied his applications for crop disaster relief and new farming loans that were routinely approved for white farmers. This wasn't right; this country must do better. He told the President and all who would listen that he wouldn't let it go.

And he hasn't. He wrote it all down. You have his remarkable story in your hands.

George Washington Hall has lived a life that he won't let vanish. He has raised a clamor that he won't let die. Thankfully, with this story, it will ring through the ages.

Roger Thurow is a journalist and author.

Chapter 1

Foundations

"Hold him, Baby! Don't give him too much slack," Mama Carrie exclaimed. "Hold him, Baby. Go with him and bring him back when he turns around. Hold him, Baby!"

I can still hear Mama Carrie's voice calling out to me, all these years later, as she coached me on how to catch this largemouth bass I had had on the fishing line. Mama Carrie was my father's mother. With her encouragement and instruction, I learned how to wear the fish down and reel it in to the bank of the pond where we both stood. Mama Carrie's eyes beamed at me with pride for having just landed such a large fish, and I felt proud of myself too. Looking back now, I can see how this fishing expedition has served as a metaphor for much of my life. I would need considerable patience, perseverance, and skill to face all that was to come.

I was born in the Deep South in Greene County, Alabama in a small town called Eutaw on February 22, 1948, to Bessie and Dencer Hall. Because I was born on President George Washington's birthday, the doctor suggested that my parents name me after him, and my mother relished the idea. Thus, I was named George Washington Hall. My parents, both natives of Greene County, acquired fifty-two acres of land on Greene County Road 133 in the late 1940s where they would farm, where our family would continue to grow, and where I now live. After me, Mamme, as we called my mother, gave birth to five other children, four boys and two girls, in all. Currently, all my siblings except Alphonso and Jimmy Lee still live.

George Hall and siblings (l-to-r): Jimmy Lee Hall, Elizabeth Hall Byrd, George Hall, Alphonso Hall, Carrie Hall Gandy

Mamme's parents were Venolia (Kimbrough) and Pearlie Smith, and Daddy's parents were Carrie (Johnson) and Liston Hall. Grandmother Venolia and Grandpa Pearlie lived around ten to fifteen miles away. While that might not sound far away today, back then with no vehicle to our names, the distance was enough to limit our time together. Mama Carrie, however, had a tremendous influence upon me. She was born in 1879 and was mother to a large family of fourteen children. Half Native American and half African American, Mama Carrie was well-acquainted with nature and possessed keen survival skills. I was her eldest grandson, and she seemed to take a special interest in me. Since Mama Carrie lived with us, we had ample opportunity to spend time together. The two of us

would roam through the woods, gathering hickory nuts, scaly bark nuts, and walnuts. During another memorable fishing expedition, I thought I had a snake on the line. However, she knew better. "Hold it, Baby! It not a snake but rather a fish." Again, with her encouragement, I reeled in that eel fish to the creek bank. I learned so much about life and gained valuable survival skills from Mama Carrie and am so grateful to her.

Daddy loved our farm—all the plants and the animals. He believed in our being as independent and self-sufficient as possible. Back then, Alabama was a hard place for Black Americans to own land and operate a farm, but my father was passionate about us owning our own land and farming. Daddy liked to hunt and fish, too. He was a great hunter and fisherman, just like Mama Carrie. Daddy was a brave and hardworking man, a World War II veteran. But after the war, he had developed cancer.

Our family always suspected his illness was due to some wartime chemical or environmental exposure. As time passed, he became sicker and sicker, and we watched in dismay as his life force ebbed away.

At age six, I entered the first grade at Cook Grade School. The following year as I began second grade, my sister Elizabeth entered first grade. At the end of the school year, Elizabeth and I were both promoted to third grade for the 1956-1957 school term. The teacher explained to my mother that if my sister and I were in the third grade together we could share the same books. She thought that as the years passed, we could save money that way.

During that school year, shortly before my ninth birthday, Daddy passed away. He was only 39 years of age when he died. Although I was still a boy of eight and was weighed down with grief, I assumed a position of leadership in my family to help my mother and my younger brothers and sisters. With six children, Mamme had a lot on her plate. Mama Carrie had nicknamed me "Man", and now it sure sounded prophetic. I helped manage the family farm. Mama Carrie assisted too. After my father passed, she would plow our fields with a mule so we could plant our crops. Both in the morning before school and in the afternoon after I returned home, I had many farm chores to help Mamme and Mama Carrie run the farm. We had no well on our property when I was young, so I carried water up to the house and farm from a stream almost a quarter of a mile away. We had a wood stove for heat and cooking, and I would carry in wood to fuel the fire. We eventually purchased a coal heater when I was around 10. We had cows, horses, and mules on our farm. Mama Carrie and I handled the bulk of the care of the livestock. We moved the animals around the property as needed for grazing and land management, and I hauled fresh water to them, and fed them hay when there was not enough fresh grass for them. Mama Carrie milked the cows every day; there is nothing quite like fresh milk! We also tended the chickens, which we kept primarily for egg production for our family, and the pigs.

In the summers when school was out, I had the whole day for work. All summer we grew crops on our land such as corn and many other varieties of vegetables. Although we were not affluent, our livestock production and produce provided good nutrition for our family. Also, on four or five acres, we planted cotton. I picked cotton for our own farm, and I also worked as a hired hand on others' farms to pick cotton and bale hay. Because I earned money when I worked for other farmers, I was able to buy my own clothes and shoes from an early age which eased the financial burden on Mamme. After Daddy died, Mamme managed the sale of our cotton in the town of Boligee where she would take it for processing and receive payment, but when I was in high school, I managed these sales, gaining valuable business skills from a young age.

Soon after my father's death, I confessed Jesus Christ as my personal Lord and Savior and joined the Jerusalem Missionary Baptist Church of the Boligee Community. My faith in Jesus Christ and His teachings have informed and guided my life ever since. My church reinforced the lessons Daddy, Mamme, and Mama Carrie labored to instill in us children. I learned about the importance of integrity and honesty, the value of hard work, the love of God for all His creation, the power of prayer, and the importance of forgiveness. Just as Jesus had forgiven those who trespassed against Him, I had to forgive those who trespassed against me. In fact, forgiving others, steadfastly loving those who behaved in unlovable ways even when it seemed impossible, remained a fixed requirement of my walk of faith. Just as God forgave me, I would be required to forgive others. I believe this practice of forgiveness proved key in maintaining my emotional groundedness through difficult trials.

Even as a child, I worked hard, but life was more than hard work. We had a lot of love in our family. I think my brothers and sisters looked up to me, and I surely loved them. Our house was near a hill, and we would climb up the hill and take turns climbing inside old car or truck tires and rolling ourselves back down the hill. Then up we would climb again to repeat the experience. What fun we had together! Also, we had an old strand of wire which we ran outside the window for an antenna. With our antenna we picked up WLAC out of Nashville and listened to gospel music together. I couldn't tell you what else was available to listen to back then. WLAC was the only station we had access to, but it was enough for us.

After a few years, Mama Carrie grew ill. She moved to Detroit, Michigan to live with her daughter, my Auntie Virginia Smith. I was in 9th or 10th grade when she left. The move was difficult on me because Mama Carrie and I had always been so close. We had worked together every day of my life, and she had been a stabilizing force in my life when Daddy had died. After she left, I took on her chores without her and her comforting presence. Auntie Virginia mailed us a few letters to keep us posted, but I never saw or spoke to Mama Carrie again. Mama Carrie finally passed away in June 1964. Mamme had bought a car during this period, and we were therefore able to visit with her parents more often. I loved them, too, but no one could fill the space in my heart and life that Mama Carrie had held.

Although the deaths of my father and my grandmother profoundly affected me, I could not give up, no matter how much I might have felt like it sometimes. My mother had insisted that I continue attending school and complete my education. She told me this was my father's express wish for me. "Your Daddy did not want you to work on no white man farm and miss school." Honoring my father, I valued education highly throughout my life. I completed third and fourth grades at Cook Grade School before the school was closed, and I entered fifth grade at Greene County Training School of Boligee, Alabama. The school has since been renamed as Paramount Junior High School. I remained at Greene County Training School for both middle and high school, graduating with my high school diploma in May 1966. I am so thankful for the positive influence of teachers in my life, particularly my math and my vocational agriculture teachers who pushed me to excel and bragged on me in class. Never underestimate the good a caring teacher can make in a young life.

School provided me with opportunities for more than just educational advancement. Through school, I gained ample experience in team sports, civic engagement, and leadership, each building my self-confidence and teaching me to work both independently and with teams. I was a member of Greene County Training School's marching band as first solo trumpeter and played on the school's baseball team.

Also, I was a member of several clubs for which several friends and classmates encouraged me to run for president. While I did not seek out these roles, I knew someone had to fill them, and if I could be of service, I would take them on. I served as President of the Future Farmers of America (FFA), President of the Student Government Association (SGA), and President of the Senior Class. Perhaps being named for our nation's first president George Washington impacted how others saw me and how I lived my life!

Chapter 2

Southern While Black

Although slavery had been abolished after the Civil War of 1861 – 1865, the United States into which I was born after World War II remained grossly unequal, despite the Constitutional Amendments which were supposedly intended to guarantee Black Americans equality. After World War II, the United States had entered into the Cold War with the USSR. Throughout this period, the United States agitated for democracy around the world even as the Soviet Union pushed communism and the expansion of Soviet power. However, even as the United States waged a Cold War against the USSR and the spread of communism in the aftermath of World War II, Black Americans were denied basic civil liberties. While discrimination occurred throughout the United States in various forms, nowhere was it more blatant and codified than in the Deep South. States in the Deep South, Alabama included, had passed the so-called Jim Crow laws which demanded Black citizens attend separate educational facilities and houses of worship, use public facilities such as bathrooms and drinking fountains labeled "for colored only", eat in separate areas from whites, and sit in the back of public transportation vehicles such as buses.[1]

The second-class treatment of Black Americans and the routine denial of their basic civil rights stood in stark contrast to the democratic picture the United States attempted to portray to the world, and the world noticed. Some Black Americans were even terrorized in their own towns and homes just for being Black.

In acts of domestic terrorism, white Americans lynched thousands of Black Americans in the hundred years following the Civil War.[2] Many more were beaten or tortured. Few were ever charged with or convicted of these crimes. A racist organization called the Ku Klux Klan burned crosses on the property of African Americans and bombed Black homes and churches to terrorize and intimidate Black Americans.[3] In fact, embarrassment over internationally publicized violence against minorities in the United States helped propel legislation to address these injustices, legislation which would vastly improve the lives of African Americans.[4] The United States could hardly afford the negative international publicity over their hypocrisy while touting the virtues of democracy.

In the spring before my entry into first grade, the Supreme Court had released its unanimous decision in Brown v. Board of Education, which overturned Plessy v. Ferguson. In 1896, the Plessy v. Ferguson decision had concluded that "separate but equal" accommodations were constitutional,[5] unleashing decades of discrimination against Black Americans who were relegated to second class citizenship and conditions that surely were separate but most certainly did not resemble equal treatment. However, on May 17, 1954, Chief Justice Earl Warren released his decision in Brown v. Board of Education of Topeka, writing: "We conclude that in the field of public education, the doctrine of 'separate but equal' has no place. Separate educational facilities are inherently unequal."[6] Nevertheless, Alabama and many other states resisted the Supreme Court's ruling for years thereafter. In fact, on March 12, 1956, nineteen U.S. Senators and eighty-two members of the U.S. House of Representatives, all from states in the former Confederacy, signed a statement called "Declaration of Constitutional Principles" in response to the Brown v. Board of

Education decision. They claimed the Supreme Court's decision was an abuse of judicial power. These senators and representatives wrote that the Supreme Court had sown "hatred and suspicion where there had been heretofore friendship and understanding" and urged Southerners to resist.[7]

Somehow, I doubt any of these representatives writing about "friendship and understanding" spoke for Black Alabamians or any other Black Southerners. Most of us had long since been disenfranchised, and our voices mattered little to our local politicians, let alone to our national ones. In any case, the Brown v. Board of Education decision had no effect on my life. I grew up in a Black community, and there were no white children in my school. Schools in Greene County, Alabama did not technically desegregate until sometime after I graduated from high school.

I was just a child and do not recall much of the adults' discussions regarding politics at the time. However, when Alabama's U.S. Senators and Representatives signed that "Declaration of Constitutional Principles", Montgomery, Alabama was amid a city-wide bus boycott, no doubt stemming from all that "friendship and understanding" that they seemed to know so much about. On December 1, 1955, a Black Alabamian woman named Rosa Parks had defied a bus driver who demanded she give up her seat to a white person. In Alabama and other Southern states, segregation laws required Blacks to sit behind whites on buses, and bus drivers often demanded Black people relinquish their seats to whites who did not find available seats when they stepped on the bus. Parks's subsequent arrest for refusing to comply led to the Montgomery Bus Boycott in which Montgomery area Black citizens refused to ride city buses during the almost thirteen-month long boycott from December 5, 1955, through

December 20, 1956. The boycott continued throughout this period as a federal district court ruled in favor of plaintiffs in a civil suit, Browder v. Gayle, who had challenged Montgomery's city ordinances requiring segregated seating on Montgomery's bus lines.[8] Furthermore, the boycott continued until the Supreme Court not only affirmed the federal district court's ruling stating that laws requiring segregated seating on public transportation were unconstitutional but also ordered the integration of the bus lines.[9]

Despite my many positive experiences at home, in church, and in school, growing up African American in Alabama impacted every aspect of my life. Discrimination and racism were inescapable, and we were very segregated from whites when I was growing up, just as the politicians who had passed the Jim Crow laws had intended. In my hometown of Eutaw, for example, the local 5-and-10 store had two drinking fountains at the back of the store. One was labeled "Colored" and the other was labeled "Whites". African Americans were considered inferior to whites by most of white society and were not permitted to drink from the water fountain designated for white people. In other places, Black Americans would not even be allowed to obtain a drink of water in the same store as white Americans. We also had an ice cream parlor in our area. Black citizens were not even allowed inside. We had to order and were served from a window at the side of the building. The movie theatre was segregated, too, by floor. Whites sat downstairs while Blacks were forced to sit upstairs in the balcony if we wanted to see a movie. And we were not permitted to use the same restroom as whites. Some places had separate facilities for Blacks and whites, but others did not, and in those cases, Blacks either had to hold it or leave to find a restroom that accepted us.

The constant degradation of African Americans weighed heavily on my soul. As a young African American, I felt helpless and had no idea how to positively impact society for fair treatment of myself and other Black Americans. However, with the confidence and skills I had gained through engaging at school and in the community, I was more than ready to participate in the battle for civil rights that was being waged throughout the South, and in Alabama especially, at this time.

During high school, I became increasingly exposed to the civil rights violations of Blacks in Alabama and across the South and to the political agitation of the period. Some of our teachers encouraged us to protest for our rights as American citizens. Lacking transportation, we protested mainly at school at first. White schools had routinely received pristine new textbooks. Black schools, like my own, were given the old worn-out textbooks as hand-me-downs when the white schools no longer wanted them. Fellow classmates and I understood clearly how these second-hand textbooks symbolized our second-class status in Alabama. We implemented a protest march at our school to bring attention to this inequity. Overall, the school and some of our teachers were incredibly supportive of our political activism. For example, during that protest, someone stuffed cotton into the keyhole of our principal's office, locking him in so he could not interfere with our demonstration. I have no idea how he was freed, but none of the students faced repercussions for that act. Perhaps he secretly approved of our passionate and principled protest strike, even if as principal he could not afford to publicly admit his support.

During my junior year of high school, many of us in our community began attending some of the weekly meetings at the First Baptist Church on Greensboro Street in Eutaw at which those gathered strategized and discussed the activities of and coordinated with the Student Nonviolent Coordinating Committee (SNCC) and Dr. Martin Luther King, Jr. as they pushed for Black voter registration and voting rights in Alabama and across the South. A group of us young men decided to attend one of the protest marches of 1965. We piled into three cars and traveled the 70 miles or so to Selma, Alabama. I drove one of the vehicles. These were scary times. We knew our attendance at the protest could be dangerous. We could be arrested and jailed. We could be beaten as other Black Americans had been. We could even be killed. In those days in the South, the freedom we as Black Americans still dreamed of was on the line. As with one of those large fish in the pond back home, I would be there to help reel in our liberty. Yes, there was trepidation. But there was also a sense of excitement. I could help my community—my people—by participating. Together we would bring much needed change to our lives and the lives of those who would come after us. And by our actions, we could honor those who had gone before us as well. I was no longer a powerless child. I was becoming a man and was standing up for what was right. In that moment, I felt pride—real pride—in myself, in my companions, and in my community.

This particular Selma demonstration of 1965 remained peaceful, and authorities did not attempt to harm us. Later Selma demonstrators, however, would face violence at the hands of the police. We felt a great sense of solidarity as we sang freedom songs and chanted in unison in favor of our voting rights. Standing side by side with so many others, doing the right thing even though it was hard, provided a sense of empowerment to us. As we returned home, our little caravan of three vehicles drove through Marengo County. The police, of course, were aware of the protests and saw us coming a mile away. They pulled over all three of our cars. The charge? Running a red light. Of course, we had assiduously obeyed the traffic laws, but it made no difference. These officers wanted to make a point about our position in Southern society. Arguing would not only have been useless, but it could also have been dangerous, even deadly. We accepted our citations and drove the long remaining miles home to Greene County and the First Baptist Church where we told those gathered all that had transpired. They enthusiastically supported us, and they passed hats around to take up a collection for our fines. Men and women chipped in their hard-earned pennies, nickels, dimes, quarters—whatever money they could—to help us. We slept that night with the peace of knowing we had the love and support of our community.

The next morning, the three of us who had driven the cars to Selma and a fourth friend drove back to the Marengo County courthouse to pay the unlawfully extracted fines. While our friend waited outside for us, we carried our coins into the courthouse in exchange for our freedom. However, an officer of the court declared that our legal tender was not legal in their courthouse. They threw us in jail. He told us that we would be released when the money was changed into greenbacks. Surely, the irony was not lost on him that we had no way to exchange the coins for dollars if we were locked in a cell and were unable to request help from anyone on the outside. Fortunately, our friend was still waiting. After some time had passed, with trepidation, he entered the courthouse to see why we were delayed in our return. The officer informed him that he would release us only when the funds we had brought in payment for the citations were converted into greenbacks. He took the coins, went to a bank to have them converted, and returned to pay the fines for us. Then the officer finally released us.

The police in Marengo had intended to demonstrate their power over us, to keep us in a state of second-class citizenship, and to intimidate us. Instead, their unrighteous actions served only to strengthen my resolve and convictions. They had falsely accused and charged us when we were innocent. Worse still, they *knew* we were innocent! They were abusing their power. Then they refused to accept coinage as legal tender in payment of the fines they had doled out to us, in effect, for pressing for our basic rights to vote as intended in the Fifteenth (and Nineteenth) Amendments of our U.S. Constitution. And they threw us in jail just because they could. Suddenly, a refrain I had often heard the elders say, "If you had made one more bale [of cotton], you would have come out" clicked. The elders were signifying the foulness of the entire system that was rigged against us as Black Americans. It seemed no matter what we did in the South, no matter how hard we worked, how diligently we followed the rules, it would never be quite enough to get ahead, because the rules could and would change on a whim to ensure that we forever came up just a little short. Nevertheless, being wrongly accused of a misdemeanor, extorted with fines, and tossed into jail over form of legal tender set the course of my life. I vowed to resist racial discrimination for the rest of my life.

Chapter 3

Uncle Sam and Me

The day after high school graduation in 1966, my sister Elizabeth and I moved to Detroit, Michigan, where we resided with Auntie Virginia on Harding Street. Auntie Virginia had visited our farm many times over the years, and we all respected and admired her. She had worked hard and had prospered in Detroit. Mamme drove Elizabeth and me to the Eutaw bus terminal that morning and hugged us both goodbye as we embarked on our 22 hour-long trip. With conflicting emotions, I boarded the Greyhound bus. The farm was my home. I loved Mamme and my brothers and sisters. I felt connected to my land and the animals and to the larger community. Yet, in Eutaw, the only way to make a living would be to pick cotton and work on the white men's farms to earn a living, and a meager one at that. If Elizabeth and I were to support ourselves, to support our own families one day, we believed we would need to strike out on our own and seek better paying work. Detroit was the place to be. Possible employment awaited, and our Auntie Virginia resided there, willing to open her arms and her home to us. Our brothers and sisters were growing up and could assume responsibility for farm chores. Elizabeth and I would find jobs and send money home to Mamme.

Around the same time, a friend from Eutaw also came to Detroit to spend the summer with some of her relatives living there. Seeing an old friend in a new place brought a bit of comfort and familiarity to us both as we adapted to our new surroundings.

We began a dating relationship. Our relationship, however, was short-lived. When her father learned that I was in Detroit and that she and I were dating, he demanded she return to Eutaw immediately.   Worried about repercussions, he had not fully supported the civil rights movement.   He believed I was too "radical" because of my involvement in the civil rights demonstrations. But I knew I had done the right thing in standing against racial discrimination and protesting for voting rights, even if there were ongoing costs associated with my actions. I had no regrets. How better to honor my ancestors? How better to provide a more just country for my future children? How else could change come?

Elizabeth landed a job at the Chrysler plant while I found work at Uniroyal Tire Company on Jefferson Avenue, building tires. With the money I earned from my employment at Uniroyal, I pursued my dream of higher education and enrolled part-time in Detroit Institute of Technology in the School of Engineering.   I knew Daddy looked down upon me from Heaven with pride.   I studied electronics part-time.

My plans screeched to a halt the day I received a draft notice that Mamme had forwarded from our home in early January 1968. I reeled from the shock and the sense that my dreams were being crushed and my goals and hard work were being thwarted. Unable to qualify for an educational deferment that was available to more affluent young men who attended college full-time, I traveled back to Alabama. Black Americans were divided in their views on service in Vietnam. The military was one of the most integrated institutions in the United States, but signs of racism throughout remained. I did not want to go to war. My father had served in World War II, and I had seen how it had affected him.

Besides, my father's dream and now my own dream for myself included a college education.

In Montgomery, I reported for duty as a conscript to the United States Army where I was reunited with one of my best childhood and lifelong friends, Earnest Edmonds. Earnest also felt unhappy about the draft. However, we faced it together. We were inducted into the army together and were assigned the same training unit and barracks. We completed basic training requirements at Fort Benning, Georgia. Although we had been drafted for two years of service, both Earnest and I volunteered for an additional year of service in hopes that we would be assigned to a field that would not require us to fight in Vietnam and which might confer greater benefits upon us after our service ended.

I found another silver lining in the draft. When I returned to Eutaw during this period, my high school sweetheart Janetta Nickson and I reunited. We had been very close for a time in high school but had broken off our relationship before graduation. Seeing her again and rekindling the sparks between us felt right. I had always admired Janetta; she was a smart woman and a genuinely good person. She wanted to be a teacher so she could help children learn. I couldn't help but to want to be with her again every chance we had. We wed quickly, and Janetta gave birth to our first child, a beautiful girl whom we named Varita, on October 5, 1968, while I was overseas.

Immediately following basic training, the U.S. Army ordered me to Fort Sill, Oklahoma where I attended Advanced Individual Training (AIT) for three months to become a radar operator repairman. They sent Earnest to helicopter school for AIT. I hoped to advance to electronics, and Earnest wanted to be a helicopter mechanic. After completing AIT, I received orders for overseas duty in South Vietnam. Crestfallen, I regretted enlisting for an additional year. After my fifteen-day leave back home in Eutaw with Janetta expired, it was with a heavy heart I said goodbye to my family and friends in Alabama for a one-year long tour of duty in the Vietnam War as an E-3, Private First Class.

The adventure commenced on an army transport flight to California and then on to Vietnam. I spent much of the trip trying to prepare myself mentally for what I would face overseas. From the air, we observed the lush green mass of jungle foliage, so different from home. Having landed, I quickly concluded that Vietnam was a strange place, and the war would be jarring to my psyche. The army fired mortar rounds at enemy lines and shells exploded. War—the real thing—differed greatly from training. But then nothing could have prepared me for war in Vietnam.

Because the enemy hid among the dense jungle territory which they knew well, the United States military was disadvantaged in battle. Therefore, the United States had decided to defoliate the forests and destroy food crops in enemy territory. Using low flying C-123's, the military sprayed an herbicide and defoliant called Agent Orange over millions of acres of Vietnam often in concentrations up to 20 times the levels recommended by the manufacturer.[10] At that time, we did not realize the extent of toxicity of dioxin—a chemical contaminant in Agent Orange—to humans.[11] Because we assumed the product was harmless to humans, troops, including myself, were often outside while aircraft dispensed Agent Orange, and it drifted over us. For many, decades would pass before the effects were identified.

One day while on my tour of duty in Vietnam, I drove from my base camp in Pleiku to collect supplies. As I drove along the highway, I passed a man who walked like my old friend Earnest. I checked the rear-view mirror and darned if he didn't look like Earnest. I stopped and reversed my vehicle. Much to my surprise and delight, Earnest and I were reunited for a brief time right there along a highway in Vietnam. We joyfully greeted one another and chatted for too short a time, as I needed to link up with a convoy so I could travel the An Khe Pass to my unit in Tuy Hoa. We regretfully said our goodbyes. We never again saw each other during our tours of duty in Vietnam, but that moment was priceless.

Vietnam changed me. I experienced and saw many unfathomable things while there. I witnessed Vietnamese people scavenging through the garbage cans of American soldiers for scraps of food discarded from our mess halls. Their poverty was so great that they appeared happy to receive whatever we tossed away. I internalized this as a lesson and have carried it close to my heart—to be thankful even for the smallest of blessings in life. However, things I saw and experienced in Vietnam also burdened me with long-term physical ailments and psychological scars. While the psychological effects were quickly obvious to me, the physical problems would not become evident for some time.

Near the end of my tour of duty in South Vietnam, I applied for missile training, and due to my technical background as a radar operator repairman and my former electronics studies, my request was granted. Under military orders, I returned to Alabama in August 1969 and was assigned to Redstone Arsenal in Huntsville, Alabama. After a fifteen-day long furlough with my family, I reported to Redstone Arsenal where I attended Missiles Electro-Mechanical Repair School. I graduated from the program, ranking third out of 21 classmates. Because of my high ranking, I was offered the position of instructor which I accepted, and next I attended military instructor school. Upon completion of training, I was assigned as a missiles electro-mechanical repairman instructor at Redstone Arsenal where I remained until I completed my three-year active-duty service. Concurrently, I continued my civilian educational goals, attending Alverson Draughon Business School in Huntsville, Alabama.

In December 1970, I received an honorable discharge from the United States Army. While the army provided me with opportunities to further my electronics training and to improve my leadership and teaching skills, the negative effects of my experience in Vietnam have continued to follow me to this day.

Having been exposed to Agent Orange while in combat in Vietnam, by the early 1990's, I had developed peripheral neuropathies affecting my arms and legs with sensations of tingling and numbness. I have also developed several other diseases linked to Agent Orange exposure including ischemic heart disease, Parkinson's disease, and diabetes mellitus type 2. Doctors, however, failed to make the connection to Agent Orange until the early 2000s. The Veterans Administration provides medical care to those of us affected.

In addition to the physical ailments incurred during my service to my country, like so many other combat veterans, I have suffered from post-traumatic stress disorder (PTSD). Nightmares plagued my nights, making sleep difficult. I still have nightmares fifty years later. During my days, I experienced intrusive memories of combat. It is no wonder why so many veterans with PTSD have turned to drugs and alcohol—anything to numb the pain and to help one forget the unforgettable. Me? I turned to what I knew best—hard work and lots of it. Hardcore workaholism was my drug of choice. By working incessantly and juggling a multitude of projects, I helped numb the pain and vanquish, at least for a time, the memories that haunted me. I was driven to always keep my mind busy—with no down time—to keep the intrusive memories somewhat at bay.

Chapter 4

New Career Opportunities

After my discharge from the U.S. Army, I moved to Bessemer, Alabama, which is about fifteen miles southwest of Birmingham where I had obtained employment with American Telephone and Telegraph Company (AT&T). I would handle frame drops, running lines inside of buildings for calls coming into plants. Janetta was pregnant with our son Alfrado at the time. While my employment plans remained unsettled, we decided that Janetta and Varita should remain close to family and friends in Eutaw where they could have strong social support. Besides, Janetta, following her own dreams, had secured regular employment as an elementary school teacher and was not free to follow me without risking her own career and seniority. Therefore, I determined within myself to also provide for them as best I could, wherever the jobs were, even if I had to sacrifice time away from my family to do so. I found it emotionally challenging to be so far from them and returned home to Eutaw on weekends and holidays to be with them.

Alfrado was born on May 27, 1971, in Eutaw while I was living in Bessemer. Around that time, I joined the 828th Transportation Battalion of the United States Army Reserve out of Andrew L. Jackson U.S. Army Reserve in Livingston, Alabama to complete my three years of active reserve following active duty. In the Reserves, we were required to train in a specified field and train in missions to stay at the ready should the President require the service of the Army Reserve for our nation's defense. I joined a military police (MP) reserve unit in Marion, Alabama and received extensive training in that field. I served with the MP reserve unit until I was recruited into the Alabama National Guard, 166th Engineer Company, on April 11, 1976. Sometime later, my National Guard unit's name was changed to 168th Engineer Company.

After completing a six-month course of study in business and computer programming at Continental Commercial College, I relocated to my hometown of Eutaw, Alabama to be with my growing family. I had hoped to land employment with Merchants and Farmers Bank in Eutaw as a computer programmer or as a loan officer. Although I qualified for these positions, I was unsuccessful in my attempts. In the early 1970s, the bank still had no Black employees, and while I could not prove the application rejection was racially motivated, racial discrimination remained entrenched in Alabama, making it difficult for Black Americans to progress professionally and to provide for their families. Therefore, I enrolled at Livingston University (currently University of West Alabama) to further my studies in business, and I continued to seek employment. I secured employment at B.F. Goodrich Tire Company in Tuscaloosa, Alabama. Once again, my studies were placed in limbo as I leapt at an opportunity to work and provide for my family.

For years, I had longed to return to farming and had repeatedly asked Mamme for a small piece of land on our family's farm to build a home for myself and my young family. Mamme had retired from farming by that point, and the land lay idle. I hated seeing the land fallow like that. Finally, shortly after gaining employment at B.F. Goodrich, my mother transferred a small piece of property to me. Janetta, Varita, Alfrado, and I continued to live in a trailer on our land while I began construction. Utilizing my knowledge of drafting, carpentry, and electrical work, I built over 90% of our home myself, saving us a considerable sum of money. With Future Farmers of America in high school, where I learned basic carpentry skills, such as how to use rulers, levels, and saws, the knowledge I had gained in the military reading schematics, and a few good books, I was well prepared for this endeavor. After framing the structure of the house with the help of friends and neighbors, I applied for a loan to the same bank which had rejected my bid for employment. They refused me the loan, so I had to fund the home construction project myself. As a family, we sacrificed greatly, foregoing any unnecessary new clothes, cars, vacations, and trips. Fortunately, I could repair our vehicles myself, and we grew much of our own food. Thus, we lived frugally.

While employed at B. F. Goodrich, I worked in manufacturing, making tires. One day, one of the hydraulic lines on the tire building machine sprayed oily fluid on the floor, unbeknownst to me. I reached for a three-foot-wide, 50 to 60-pound roll of inner lining tire material and slipped on the oily floor. In the fall, I sustained a serious back injury. For several months, I was laid up with a back brace, followed by a lengthy round of physical therapy. In the interim, I was forced to quit my job. However, remaining idle has never been an option for me. I needed to keep active. Therefore, as soon as I was well enough, I enrolled at C.A. Fredd Technical College in Tuscaloosa to study electronics. Later I transferred to Shelton State Community College's Technical Division. The two schools were eventually consolidated in 1994. As a veteran and Army Reserve member, I received a stipend for schooling under the GI bill, so even if I were not working, I could continue to grow professionally and chip away at my long-term goal of a college degree. Concurrently, I started farming excess vegetables for sale to make ends meet and support my children. I felt compelled to take or make any work I could to provide for them.

Eventually, after my back had healed enough for me to return to full-time work, I secured employment as a communication officer (dispatcher) with the Eutaw Police Department in 1973. This job required no heavy lifting and would allow me entry into a career in law enforcement. Because I worked swing shifts, it became impossible for me to continue my studies at Shelton State Community College. However, even as that door

closed, my work as a communication officer opened new doors. I soon became a police officer with the City of Eutaw. As a job requirement, upon acceptance of the position, I enrolled in the University of Alabama Minimum Standard School to obtain certification as a police officer.

Although conditions in Alabama had improved over the previous ten years, discrimination and prejudice were still rampant. While serving as a police officer in Eutaw, the city police department attempted to continue a level of segregation. White police were expected to police white areas and Black police were assigned primarily to Black areas. The department strongly discouraged Black officers from ticketing white citizens. As a Black officer, I was discouraged from arresting whites for drinking and driving infractions and the like but was encouraged to arrest Blacks for the same crimes and misdemeanors. A young Black adult and a young white adult might commit the same crime, but only the Black youth would be ticketed and receive a police record. Whites would often be released with only a warning. This inequity in the criminal justice system resulted in Blacks having a disproportionate number of police records which would follow them throughout their lives, making it more difficult for those Black citizens to find meaningful work. After having demonstrated for our voting rights and to end discrimination, it was discouraging to see how deeply embedded institutional racism remained in Alabama. In fact, I would witness this racism play out in the way law enforcement, the courts, the public, and the media treated minorities versus white Americans during the War on Drugs of the 1980s. African Americans were viewed as criminals and addicts while white Americans were portrayed as victims of drug dependencies. Furthermore, crack cocaine use and distribution, being associated with Black Americans, were punished much more harshly than powdered cocaine use and distribution, which were more often associated with white Americans.[12]

During this period, I became a member of King Solomon Masonic Lodge #272A of Eutaw, Alabama. The masonic lodge was a Christian-based organization which allowed men to develop strong relationships with each other based on brotherhood and brotherly love. In the masonic lodge, we shared ideas, discussed various points of view and opinions on a multitude of issues. We were able to depend upon each other. Strong ties and a sense of brotherhood were among the admirable qualities of military life, and I rediscovered some of those attributes within the Freemasons. The masons also maintained an outreach to our families and the wider community. We hosted many functions such as dinners, ballgames, and other activities in which we would invite our wives and families. I continued my progress through the masons and became a Worshipful Master of the lodge. As Worshipful Master, I presided over the lodge's rituals and ceremonies and chaired business committees. While I devoted myself to the Freemasons because of my love for and commitment to the community, I gained additional leadership skills because of my membership and service.

Chapter 5

Shattering Glass Ceilings

Under a federal court order, the State of Alabama had hired its first three African American state troopers in March of 1972. Federal District Judge Frank M. Johnson, Jr. ordered the Alabama Department of Public Safety to hire one Black officer for each white officer hired until the state police force became 25% Black, to match the proportion of Blacks in Alabama.[13] One of those three officers was assigned to Greene County, and he and I met and became friends. He was the one who informed me that the state needed more Black troopers. He also told me that it was rumored that Blacks found passing the entrance examination difficult. I already worked as a city police officer and had experience as a military police officer, so I accepted this as a personal challenge and as a potential opportunity to better support my family. I took and easily passed the entrance examination.

In October 1975, I accepted an offer of employment with the Alabama State Troopers, and I attended the Alabama Police Academy in Montgomery, Alabama. I vowed never to forget the treatment my friends and I had received at the hands of police after the demonstration in Selma in 1965. Serving as a state police officer, I believed, would allow me to make a difference in how Black citizens were treated. I would try to influence fair and respectful treatment of all citizens, including Black Americans. Most of my fellow officers on the state police force were white, of course, since the court order demanding an end to racial discrimination against African Americans in law enforcement hiring had not been in effect long enough to significantly alter the racial composition of the state police force, and even when the court order was fulfilled, the proportion would likely not exceed the twenty-five percent required by law. Still, among state troopers, a brotherhood existed which overrode some of the discrimination and prejudice witnessed among the wider population. As police officers, we had one another's backs. Nevertheless, white state troopers received better details (work assignments) than Black officers.

I was assigned as a State Trooper in Greenville in Butler County where I remained in service for four years. Greenville was over 120 miles from my home in Eutaw. Again, I was separated from my family who remained in Eutaw at our home. Being such a distance from my family was hard on all of us, and I returned home as often as possible on my days off to be with my wife and children whom I loved so much. Originally, I thought the assignment in Greenville would be short-lived, and I would be assigned work in Greene County at some point, so accepting the position in Greenville had made sense.

However, throughout that period, I repeatedly requested transfers to be closer to home to no avail.

Finally, I informed my captain that I planned to resign from the Alabama State Troopers so I could be with my family. The captain seemed shocked that I might quit, and I was surprised when he told me that he did not want me to resign because he thought I was one of the more outstanding troopers at that post. As a state trooper over the previous four years, I had gained the respect of my fellow state troopers, the court system, and the public I served. I had always endeavored to be firm but fair and kind in the performance of my duties. In fact, numerous citizens wrote letters commending my professionalism. Apparently, none of this had escaped the captain's notice. My captain had not informed higher command of my requests for transfers, and I had therefore not been given consideration for reassignment all this time. However, when the captain realized how serious I was about resigning to be close to my family, he asked me to give him a little time to see what he could do. The captain contacted the colonel of the Highway Patrol Division at the Alabama State Troopers office in Montgomery, Alabama, and informed him that I planned to resign if I was not assigned to my home area in Greene County. He requested that they reassign me quickly so they would not lose me. The colonel explained to me that they could not assign me to Greene County at that time because there was already a Black trooper assigned there. On the other hand, they needed Black troopers in Sumter County which was adjacent to Greene County. He then offered me an assignment in Sumter with a promise of a transfer as soon as possible to Greene County. I accepted this offer. While this assignment would still not have me home in Eutaw with my family every day, I could see them more often and for longer periods. Besides, they promised me it would not be long until I would be stationed in Greene County.

Unfortunately, the sergeant who became my supervisor in Sumter County was not like my captain in Greenville. He seemed racist and did not seem to like me or other Black officers. He would routinely harass Black troopers for any violations in submitted paperwork, standard of dress, or vehicle maintenance. He did not harass white troopers for similar real or imagined violations nearly as much. Fortunately, I was no longer on probation as a rookie and was well-established after four years of service with the State Troopers, and I had the respect of other officers and written proof of the respect of citizens with whom I had worked. My former service in the military had taught me much about respect and discipline and how to work towards the completion of goals without becoming sidetracked. I policed by the book and complied with all rules and regulations.

However, a short time after being assigned to Sumter County, another Black trooper was assigned there fresh out of troopers' academy. The rookie was placed under my supervision. I noticed that the sergeant seemed to be harassing the rookie. I knew what the sergeant was capable of and the various pitfalls a rookie needed to avoid, so I took him under my wing and coached him on how to submit proper documentation. The sergeant became agitated that he did not have enough reasons to find fault with the rookie. He confronted me and accused me of doing the rookie's work for him and told me that I needed to let him make more mistakes. Although I explained to the sergeant that I did not perform any of the rookie's work and merely coached him as his supervisor on how to make sure his work met all standards, the sergeant did not believe me and remained angry with me. I felt stuck in the middle, but I refused to sit by and allow the rookie to be railroaded by this racist sergeant. Nevertheless, I felt stressed by the increasingly tense relationship with my direct supervisor. Eventually, I felt confident that the rookie knew his job and all the rules well enough to stand on his own despite the sergeant's racist attitudes and behaviors.

At that point, I decided it was time for me to resign from the state troopers. My record was spotless, and I did not want to jeopardize my standing within the police force by further conflict with the sergeant. It seemed only a matter of time before he found something to use against me. In addition, another year had passed, and they had failed to assign me to Greene County. I could not continue living apart from my family. Therefore, I accepted a position as police officer with City of Eutaw Police Department. Finally, I was moving back home to Eutaw where my heart had long remained.

Reflecting on my experience with the state troopers, I perceived that even in the late 1970s racism reared its ugly head. The culture had not changed nearly enough. In addition to white troopers receiving better work assignments and my experience with the racist sergeant in Sumter County, Black troopers were expected to arrest and give citations to Black people but to look the other way when whites committed similar offenses. White troopers would let whites off the hook for crimes and violations they would hold Blacks accountable for. Some troopers were so corrupt that they would target Blacks for nonexistent violations and arrest them. Fortunately, there were other officers who maintained positive attitudes toward Blacks and treated them fairly. I was especially impressed with one white officer who had also been in the military as I had been and appeared to have shed the old racist Southern attitudes. He consistently attempted to do the right thing by both Blacks and whites, wherever he served.

Returning to Eutaw as a city police officer in 1979 did allow me more time with my family which we had all longed for. I easily transitioned to family life since I had routinely returned home on weekends and other days off. When I was not policing, I found working our five acres of land to be a healing balm for my soul. Policing is an inherently demanding and stressful job in which we too often witness the worst in people. Some police officers develop alcohol abuse disorder because the job puts so much pressure on them. However, working and improving the land which I loved so much provided me with an outlet for pent up stress in my body and soul. The farm grounded and connected me with my father and grandmother who had passed away so many years before. As soon as I returned home from a shift of police work, I would jump directly to farm work. Farming required a great deal of clearheaded planning which kept my mind occupied. Sometimes Janetta, Varita, and Alfrado would assist, and we would work together as a family. I believed farming to be a positive and constructive means of channeling my time and energy, providing us with wholesome nutrition, slashing our food budget, and keeping the worst of my PTSD experiences at bay.

In 1980, I was ordained as a deacon of the Jerusalem Missionary Baptist Church in Greene County, not far from home, where I had first come to Christ. My belief in Jesus Christ had remained strong, and Christ and His teachings continued to be the cornerstone of my life. Service to the community of faith was an honor. As a deacon, I could help others in my congregation in their Christian walk and could hopefully serve as a role model of a strong Black man of faith to both other adults and to the youth. As a deacon, I assisted in devotional services and led prayer and worship—singing songs of praise to Jesus—taught adult Sunday school classes, assisted in the financial oversight of the church, and maintained the physical property. We held services every other Sunday. The church and my spiritual connection with the Lord fed my soul. As a deacon and a man of God, I felt a strong conviction that my life should serve as a model for others, an example as to how one should conduct himself in daily life. I modeled care for the less fortunate and tried to cheer the discouraged. Along with other leaders in the church, I helped other believers improve their own lifestyles so they could enjoy the benefits and spiritual blessings of living right with the Lord. Among the most important of Jesus's teachings is "Do unto others as you would have them do unto you." Jesus's message of love and forgiveness continued to give me the strength to forgive the racism and injustices I witnessed and experienced in the South. Without the Lord, I might have burned with anger or succumbed to grief after the "pennies in the courthouse" incident, my Vietnam War experience, and my experiences on the police force. As it was, I would face much more and would lean heavily upon the Lord through trials to come.

In 1982, I entered the political arena and campaigned for the position of Sheriff of Greene County. The City of Eutaw Police Department, where I worked as a police officer, covered only misdemeanors within the Eutaw city limits. The city was predominantly white at the time. Boligee, a much smaller town, had only one or two officers who covered misdemeanors within Boligee town limits. The Sheriff's office, on the other hand, covered the rest of Greene County. In addition, any felonies committed in Eutaw or Boligee fell under the jurisdiction of the Sheriff's Office. With my years of experience in the military, with the military police, as state trooper and as a City of Eutaw police officer, I believed I had something to offer in law enforcement service to our local community. Consumption of illicit drugs was far too prevalent in the United States in the early 1980s, and health and law enforcement officials and the public were becoming increasingly alarmed. Drug abuse in the United States was often portrayed as primarily a Black American problem, but as a police officer, I knew that white Americans were abusing drugs in similar or even higher proportions. Regardless of race, I believed I could have an impact on curtailing drug abuse and other crimes in Greene County. There were several Democrats running for the position in 1982. I had won the primary vote, but because none of us had received over 50% of the vote, the other leading candidate and I faced each other in a run-off. The vote count was close; I lost by fewer than 300 votes.

Chapter 6

Farming While Black

Meanwhile, after working our small family farm for a year or two, I developed a plan not only to improve our land, but to expand our farming operation. With one hundred acres, I reasoned, we could raise beef cattle as a profitable farming enterprise, grow corn and hay for their winter feed, and produce sweet potatoes, turnip and collard greens, and peas for sale. In 1982, I purchased one hundred acres of farmland across the interstate and about a mile from our home and existing farm, as well as farm equipment and livestock. In some ways, what should have been one of the biggest blessings of my and my family's lives became a curse as I entered into a business agreement for the first time with the United States Department of Agriculture (USDA) and their Farmer's Home Administration (FmHA). At first, the loan officer seemed helpful. However, he in fact offered me the bare minimum of assistance and set me up for failure. First, the loan officer would not allow me to purchase the land with its value as its own collateral. While I believed it was obvious if I could not pay back the loan for the land that the land would be repossessed by the bank while still retaining its full value, the loan officer disagreed and insisted that I use our home as additional collateral to secure the loan. As I would later discover, the FmHA rarely required this type of overcollateralization from whites but routinely demanded overcollateralization from Black farmers. We owned our home outright since Mamme had gifted us the land, and I had built the house myself, so this was a huge risk for us. We had also purchased equipment such as a tractor and cultivator, hay baler, hay conditioner and rakes against our home. Despite the setback, we were still on course for a successful cattle farming operation. Then the loan officer refused to allow me to purchase the livestock with the balance of equity in my home. By my initial reckoning, I would need to sell thirty to forty head of cattle a year to make the note payments on the farm loan. Without funds to purchase an initial herd of cattle, we were at risk of losing not just the new land and equipment, but the land Mamme had given us and the home we had worked so hard to build.

As a farmer, I appreciated the agricultural expertise available to me via the Cooperative Extension Services and worked closely with their representatives at both Tuskegee University and Auburn University to make use of the most up-to-date scientific information available. In February 1983, I was selected by Tuskegee University as an Outstanding Small Farmer in Alabama and was awarded the Merit Farm Family Award in recognition of achievements in application of science to farm and home. A university committee selected its award recipients based on data supporting the farmer's accomplishments over the past year. Over the previous years, I had developed relationships with the representatives of both the Tuskegee and the Auburn cooperative extension services offices in Greene County and continued to work in cooperation with them for years thereafter.

The Greene County Tuskegee extension service agent, Lucious H. Rodgers, was also a Black American. Like me, he understood the specific needs of Black farmers in the South. Together, we organized the Greene County Farmers' Self-Help Cooperative. I served as the organization's president until 1990. The mission of our cooperative was to provide a common marketplace and associated resources for local farmers to sell their fruits and vegetables and other farm products rather than relying on consumers to travel to individual farms. Most of our members had only a few acres on which they grew rows of vegetables, so they could really benefit from collective actions. We had around twenty-five to thirty members at any one time, mostly Black farmers. Only a couple white farmers joined. Many whites still did not wish to work closely with Blacks as equals in the 1980s in Alabama.

Rodgers recognized my need to obtain cattle quickly and inexpensively and suggested I reach out to Heifer International to acquire top quality beef cattle for myself and other small farmers in our cooperative. Heifer International, based in Little Rock, Arkansas, aims to reduce poverty and hunger throughout the world by supporting farmers and farming initiatives. Heifer International provided cows to prospective cattle farmers participating in our project. In turn, as the cattle reproduced, the cattle farmers would pass on the same number of cows they had received to other farmers to help them begin their own herds. Alternatively, if they found no recipients interested in the offspring, they could sell that same number of cattle over the next couple of years and give the proceeds back to Heifer International. Heifer International granted me ten head of cattle with which to build my herd, and over the following three years, I gifted a total of ten cows to several different farmers interested in small scale cattle farming. Since these were all small farms—only ten to fifteen acres of land—they could accept only a couple of cows each.

While Heifer International remains an excellent organization and provided me much needed support in my beef cattle farming endeavors, it took me several years to build up a herd and become profitable since the FmHA refused to lend me funds to purchase the cattle I initially needed to meet the goals outlined in my business plan. The USDA through the local FmHA office proceeded to undermine my agricultural operations through other underhanded techniques. Farmers routinely borrow funds at the outset of the growing season to purchase supplies and to manage cash flow as they pay hired workers before the crops are harvested and sold. Continuing to work through our county's FmHA office, I applied for loans, but the FmHA would often approve the loans late. When funds failed to arrive until late in the growing season, we would have to rush to plant before the deadline, and crops would often fail. Certainly, no bumper crops were possible when loans arrived late because the best part of the growing season had passed. By way of example, corn crops in Alabama needed to be planted by March and other crops needed to be planted just a little later in April to benefit from the spring rains and for the growing season to be productive. When my funds came beyond that time, later than the white farmers' loan approvals, I would be handicapped in producing a profitable harvest.

As I was to discover later, these tactics were not directed at me alone, but Black farmers throughout the South were experiencing similar treatment from our local USDA offices. Often when Black farmers applied for loans, there would be delays in approving them.[14] When Black farmers would inquire as to the disposition of their loans, they would learn that their paperwork "had not been received" or that their applications were still "being processed." Loans were denied, or only partially approved for Black farmers throughout this period. Funds arrived late in the growing season.[15] Like me, other farmers were being denied disaster relief that was granted to white farmers or having their disaster relief reduced. Although the USDA in Washington, D.C. had no policy actively promoting the discrimination of Black farmers, the USDA failed to provide adequate oversight of their employees and offices in the states and their counties. The USDA hired local people in their states and counties to implement their programs, plans and policies. Local people brought their local prejudices with them. Each county had a Farmer's Home Administration office, and farmers would work with those local representatives of the USDA with all their prejudices, for better or worse.

Each county also had a U. S. Agriculture Consolidated Farmer's Service Agency (FSA) Committee which would work with the local

FmHA USDA office. Local citizens, elected by the local community, comprised the FSA committee. Representation on the committee, however, was rarely representative of the community. Only land-owning farmers could vote. Greene County, for example, was between 80%-90% African American at the time, but most of the land was owned by whites. Therefore, whites still maintained the majority voting rights in these election processes, and they voted overwhelmingly for other whites to serve on the committee. In addition, Black farmers were often excluded from the process by whatever means possible. For example, the local FmHA office failed to alert Black farmers on the voting process or to send out the necessary paperwork to Black farmers in a timely manner for them to take advantage of their voting rights. I myself did not learn about the process until I started filing complaints about the discriminatory treatment I had received from FmHA. Even knowing the process and their rights, Black farmers were often reticent to oppose the system the local FmHA and FSA committees had established because they remained at the mercy of the local FmHA office for their loans and other farm programs and support, and when they did vote, Black farmers were discouraged from voting against the whites who ran for the FSA committee because they remained financially dependent upon the powerful white families in the community.

Chapter 7

EEOC Complaint Against the City of Eutaw

In the interim, in the summer of 1984, the position of Assistant Chief of Police of the City of Eutaw became vacant. Chief Rhodes had retired from the force, and in August 1984, Assistant Chief of Police Vernie Stripling was appointed Chief of Police.[16]   I expressed my interest in the position of Assistant Chief of Police, but Vernie's brother Dennis Stripling was hired for the position.[17] There was no known selection process. I approached Chief Vernie Stripling about the promotions, challenging the decision and the fact that I had not been considered, but he told me he had nothing to do with the procedure and indicated that the appointments had been made by a four-member committee which included the Mayor of Eutaw, Joe L. Sanders.[18] I filed a complaint with the Equal Employment Opportunity Commission (EEOC) regarding what I believed to be a discriminatory process since a less qualified Caucasian male was appointed by the Council with no opportunity offered for highly qualified African Americans to be fairly considered. I had ample experience that had prepared me well for the position of Assistant Chief.   I had attended minimum standards training, worked as a police dispatcher, attended the Alabama State Police Academy, and served as an Alabama state trooper. I also had extensive military experience having served in the U.S. Army, the U.S. Army Reserve, and the National Guard, and

I had trained as military police. I believed I had been discriminated against.

The EEOC investigated my complaint. The EEOC upheld the City of Eutaw's hiring decision since the city had published no policy and procedure manual for the Eutaw Police Department as to how vacant positions were to be filled. Therefore, in the EEOC's opinion, they had not violated any policies. However, as an outcome of the EEOC's investigation, the City of Eutaw was required to develop a personnel policy and procedure manual which would apply to all employees. The City Council approved the resolution on August 12, 1986. Despite the development of the new manual, the EEOC ruling did not feel like much of a victory. Perhaps it was the best decision they could make at the time based on their own policies, but it seemed an all too convenient way to avoid making a clear decision regarding right versus wrong. The good old boys' network had triumphed. I did find myself wondering if the EEOC avoided calling the hiring "discriminatory" because I would then have had justification for filing a lawsuit, but as with so many other individual actions, such suspicions are hard to prove.

Throughout the process, I stood alone. None of the Eutaw police officers lent me support, not even the other African Americans who comprised a minority of the police force. Most people will not complain about unfair treatment for fear of repercussions. Fortunately, I did not face any obvious repercussions from filing the EEOC complaint, but there were hard feelings. The City Council at the time was all white, and it would be years before those in positions of authority at that time would be voted out of office or retire. In the interim, the City of Eutaw Police and other agencies fulfilled minimum requirements.

Otherwise, they behaved the same towards Black citizens, as far as I could tell.

Chapter 8

Farm Expansion and Bankruptcy

In 1985, I expanded my farming operation to include the production, manufacturing, and marketing of homemade sorghum and ribbon cane syrups under the trademarked Hall's Homemade Syrup label. My uncle Nelson Smith farmed across the highway from my family's farm. He had been producing a small amount of ribbon cane on a third of an acre for some time but had recently found it difficult to harvest and sell since ribbon cane and syrup had fallen out of favor for use in sugar production in the 1960s.[19] Around 70% of refined sugar and cane syrup have been derived from sugar cane since then, with beet sugar making up the remainder of refined sugar production.[20] Uncle Nelson offered me all his ribbon cane if I wanted it. I thought ribbon cane syrup would be an excellent addition to my farming enterprises as an artisanal product. Since the process of growing and processing ribbon cane into syrup had become almost extinct, being part of a small contingent of farmers keeping the tradition alive appealed to me. Ribbon cane syrup has a fuller, richer flavor than sugar cane syrup. Some people still prefer it despite the ever-increasing preference among Americans for sweetness.

Ribbon cane is grown from eyes on the cane and takes time and care to propagate. Ribbon cane is an annual crop, planted in early spring and harvested in late autumn. An acre of cane can yield a couple hundred gallons of syrup. Within a few years, I had grown a substantial quantity of ribbon cane with which to begin my syrup production operations. I contacted an elder—a retired syrup maker—who traveled to my farm to teach me how to cook the ribbon cane to produce the ribbon cane syrup myself. I took great pride in growing the raw cane product without herbicides, pesticides, or other chemicals. I processed the syrup naturally by open evaporation through a cooking process without any additives or preservatives. I maintained quality by analyzing the sugar content of the finished product and by working closely with Tuskegee University and the Cooperative Extension Service which would perform laboratory analysis on the nutritional values before labeling. It felt good to see my name and logo on the label of a product I had created and could be proud of.

For many years, I marketed the syrup production as an agritourism opportunity. I also utilized it as a form of community outreach. From September through November, teachers would bring their students on field trips to the plant to learn about syrup production. Elderly citizens from nearby nursing homes would also tour the facilities. I got a kick out of watching the amazement on their faces as they saw syrup produced. Most people had previously only seen the product on store shelves and had had no idea what was involved in its production. Due to my current health concerns, I cannot produce much now, but syrup production remains near and dear to my heart, so I still produce a small amount for mail orders and for local people who are willing to drive to the processing plant for pick up.

After a few years of insufficient farm profits to make the required loan payments to FmHA due to crop disasters and the limited herd of cattle with which I was forced to work, my account became delinquent. I approached the FmHA officers to request assistance in restructuring my loan by developing a new plan that would improve my business's cash flow and enable me to make payments on the loan. They refused. The local FmHA officers seemed to want my farm to fail. They had a possible motive. If my farm failed, my property would go up for auction and a richer white person could purchase it possibly at a reduced rate, and I would lose all the equity I had accrued in my property. Again, as I would later learn, this is exactly what was happening to Black farmers in many states during this period. Minority farm ownership was in crisis. Over the course of the 20th century, African American farm ownership had declined dramatically from

14% of all farms in 1920 to only 1% of farms in 1992.[21] African American farmland ownership had reached its zenith in 1910 at 16,000,000 to 19,000,000 acres but had declined to only 1,500,000 acres by 1997 according to the USDA Census of Agriculture.[22] Many of these farm losses were due to underhanded or fraudulent practices used to wrest land from African Americans and into white hands. And I was in danger of becoming one more African American farmer to lose his land.

In fact, the United States government had precipitated a larger crisis in small-scale farming during the first half of the 1970s which rippled through the following decades. From 1971-1976, Earl Butz served as Secretary of Agriculture under President Richard Nixon and President Gerald Ford.[23] Besides his notoriety for vulgar, obscene, racist, and anti-Catholic remarks, Secretary Butz may have been best known for his "get big or get out" dictum to United States farmers. Under his federal policies favoring big agriculture, policies which the United States continued to promote long after, small-scale family farm operations became financially unstable, and many farmers faced bankruptcy or were otherwise forced out of agriculture.[24] These policies undoubtedly affected Black farmers disproportionately since Black farmers tended to own smaller farms. However, the larger issue for Black farmers was the racial discrimination perpetrated by the USDA through the FmHA and the local Farm Service Administration Committee boards. Local white committee members did not want Black farmers to be successful and few financial institutions would finance Black farmers with the large capital loans of millions of dollars that would have allowed them to "get big."

Others had noticed this trend. During the farming crisis of the 1980s, journalists began reporting on the disproportionate losses Black farmers faced. For example, on Tuesday, April 29, 1987, New York Newsday published an article entitled "They're Losing the Land." This article captured the misfortunes several Black farmers had suffered with FmHA, including myself and Tim Pigford of North Carolina, whom I did not know at the time. In fact, Tim and I would meet years later and join efforts in our fight against racial discrimination in farming. In an excerpt from that New York Newsday article, entitled "1 Man's Struggle," Dallas Gatewood reported on an interview he had conducted with me about some of the difficulties I had had with my local FmHA office. He noted that I was facing foreclosure on my 250-acre farm after years of drought and the resulting poor crop yields which had caused us to fall behind on loan payments. Gatewood wrote that Janetta and I could lose our house and land and that the FmHA had refused my proposal for a debt restructuring package. The FmHA had set our living expenses at an unreasonably high rate, considering we had almost no actual food expenses since we provided for our family's food needs by farming. It became clear that my struggle with the FmHA as a Black farmer was just a microcosm of a systemic issue within the USDA and FmHA. Evidence mounted that the FmHA used unethical tactics throughout the South and continued to seize Black owned farmland in over-collateralized loan foreclosures.

With my farm and property at risk, I spent considerable time in prayer. One day, I shared my predicament with a friend, a white Canadian farmer who grew soybeans locally. He suggested I consider filing for bankruptcy rather than default on the loan. According to his knowledge, if I filed bankruptcy, the courts would work with me on a repayment plan. If I met that commitment, the USDA would not be able to touch my land for a period of ten years.

I hired an attorney who confirmed this was true. Thanks be to God; I now had a way out. With a mixture of sadness and gratitude, I filed for personal bankruptcy. Through the bankruptcy, I wound up under the umbrella of the court. The court considered all my financial obligations. They considered the equipment I owned and wrote off any that was deemed to have met its ten-year useful life expectancy according to rules for depreciation. Then the court established a realistic repayment plan for the loans. Regardless of how perturbed the FmHA officials might be, this was one African American owned farm they would not get their hands on, at least not for the next ten years. Still, the mistreatment I had received by the FmHA reminded me of the incident with the pennies supposedly not being legal in the courthouse in that different standards were applied to Blacks than to whites and how the system remained cruelly unfair to Black Americans.

Chapter 9

Fair Promotion

Throughout this period, I continued to feel the urging of the Spirit to become Sheriff of Greene County. Holding firm to my dream, I campaigned for the position a second time in 1986. Again, I won the primary but not by a large enough percentage to avoid a run-off. I was once again defeated in the run-off election by fewer than 300 votes. Though disappointing, the run-off results were fair. Apparently, the time was not yet right. But the third time is the charm. In 1990, I campaigned for the position of sheriff and won by an overwhelming margin against six opponents. No run-offs! Then I went on to win the election. I imagined Mama Carrie smiling down from heaven upon me. Once again, I had held on and reeled in a dream, just as she had taught me. Quickly, I settled into the role of sheriff, attempting to police fairly and by the book. The citizens in my county deserved fairness and integrity in a sheriff, and I would give them these.

However, politics and racism bled over into the National Guard where I had served for a decade and a half. In the mid to late 1980s, the Guard overlooked me for promotion from Staff Sergeant (E-6) to Sergeant First Class (E-7). While I strongly believed I should have been considered for this promotion and was discouraged that I had not been given consideration, the one silver lining was that my long-time friend SFC Earnest Edmonds received the promotion from E-6 to E-7.[25] It occurred to me that my 1984 EEOC complaint against the City of Eutaw may have offended some of my superiors in the Alabama National Guard. I was the sort of person to challenge the system when it was unjust. They did not seem to appreciate that kind of behavior from a Black man. Then, in 1992, while I served as Sheriff of Greene County, the Alabama National Guard again gave me no consideration for promotion from E-6 to E-7. They filled the vacancy in the 168th Engineer Company without following promotion criteria as outlined in National Guard Regulation 600-200, Section IV, Paragraphs 6-29, 6-30, and 6-34.[26] SFC Frank Lewis received the promotion.[27] I believed I should have had an equal shot, having served in the U.S. Army, the U.S. Army Reserve, and the Alabama National Guard for twenty-four years and having served my state and local communities in law enforcement for nearly two decades.

The National Guard seemed to maintain a "good old boy" system. They did as they pleased, as evident in their failure to follow promotion criteria in NGR 600-200. They tended to promote their friends. All the high positions in the Alabama National Guard were held by whites, most of whom had never served in active duty. Many whites had joined the Alabama National Guard as a way of avoiding the Vietnam War. In the 1960s, the Alabama National Guard provided a haven from war for white men while Black men went overseas to fight. Most of the Blacks in the Alabama National Guard had served in the United States Armed Forces but once in the Guard, their promotions came only slowly, if at all. As for me, I think my open complaints about the lack of promotions for African Americans rankled them, as did my position of authority as sheriff in Greene County. I was unafraid of the good old boy network.

After being denied consideration for promotion a second time, I complained to the commander in charge. He appeared uninterested in rectifying the injustice or in their failure to follow the prescribed regulations regarding promotions. Therefore, I filed a complaint in September 1992 with the Alabama National Guard Command. I received no response.

On November 29, 1992, I reached out to my U.S. Senator Richard Shelby and to my Congressional Representative Claude Harris, Jr. Representative Harris had declined to run for another term, and he suggested I wait until sometime after Congress reconvened in January 1993, at which point, I should contact his successor, Representative Earl Hilliard.[28] In February 1993, I visited the Inspector General's office in Montgomery, Alabama. While

there, I spoke with Colonel Edgar L Smith, III. He outlined several steps as to how this complaint should be resolved. Colonel Smith would see that the complaint was forwarded to Colonel Powell, Commander of 145th Engineering Battalion in Montgomery, Alabama.[29] I recall no guarantees that the situation would be resolved to my satisfaction.

I continued applying pressure to the situation through my U.S. congressional representative. Taking Rep. Claude Harris's advice, I reached out to Rep. Earl Hilliard. He sent his press secretary to meet with me at the office of Governor Jim Folsom, Jr. I had thought we might meet with the Governor himself, but his assistant met with us instead. I informed him of all that had transpired regarding my complaint in twice being overlooked for promotion and how the Alabama National Guard had done so in violation of the National Guard regulations. The assistant assured Rep. Earl Hilliard's press secretary and me that the matter would be resolved appropriately.

A few days later, Governor Folsom sent a sergeant major with the Alabama National Guard from Montgomery to meet with me in Greene County. We discussed the situation at length. One thing about that discussion especially remains in my mind. The sergeant major wanted to know why I had not contacted the Alabama National Guard Command before I turned to my congressional representatives. I informed him that I had indeed gone to the Alabama National Guard Command first but that they had given no response to my accusation. The fact that he had no knowledge that I had followed proper protocol saddened me and underscored the importance of my escalating my complaint to my representatives. If I had not doggedly pursued this complaint, I doubt it would have seen the light of day where the injustice of it could be properly disinfected. What is hidden in the darkness, must be brought to light, if there is to be any change in this world. The sergeant major assured me that I would receive my promotion.

In the interim, in response to an inquiry from Senator Shelby, Major General James E. Moore replied by letter that a promotion board would convene and reconsider all soldiers who were originally qualified at that time for promotion. Later, when I spoke with Commander Colonel Lamb about the status of my complaint, he advised me that the promotion board would convene in April to discuss projected vacancies. They, however, would not reconsider prior discrepancies such as the one my complaint had been about.[30] They had no intention of removing SFC Lewis from his position. I learned that if I were promoted, I would have to accept a position wherever the vacancy existed in the battalion. Chances were high that I would receive my long-awaited promotion to E-7 but that it would be in another unit some distance away, meaning that once again, I would need to be away from my home, family, the sheriff's office, and the farm. This was unacceptable to me. The Guard had had six months by this time to resolve my original complaint. Disappointed in the system, I immediately alerted Rep. Earl Hilliard's office as to the new developments and requested a full investigation. Shortly thereafter, I appeared before the Sergeant First Class Promotion Board. I anxiously awaited the Board's decision and pondered what my response should be if they did indeed attempt to promote me outside my unit.

Concurrently, I had remained a student at Stillman College. In 1993, I had been assigned a dilemma project in which one is faced with a choice between unsatisfactory alternatives. Living this real-life dilemma in the Alabama National Guard, I felt the situation would be a perfect case study for my class assignment. I presented my dilemma on the Alabama National Guard, their action toward me, and what possible recourse I would have. A major in the United States Army Reserve in Camp Shelby, Mississippi was a classmate at Stillman. He and I had grown to respect each other over the course of our studies, and he had told me at one point that if I wanted, he could get me back into the Army Reserves. The major was another one of the friends I have made upon my life's journey who truly judged people by their character and competence rather than by the color of their skin. One day, he phoned me because he was curious to see how my situation with the Alabama National Guard had developed since we had last seen each other and if I had received my promotion. I advised him that I had not received my promotion, but I had recently appeared before the promotion board and was awaiting their decision. Again, the major asked me if I would like to rejoin the United States Army Reserve. He assured me that he could offer me an E-7 slot for promotion. It seemed likely to me that the Alabama National Guard would offer me an E-7 at this point, but it would probably be a long time before I would be promoted again to an E-8 even though if they had treated me fairly, I would already have been an E-8. I asked the major if the Alabama National Guard promoted me to E-7, would he be able to offer me an E-8 slot? The major answered in the affirmative. Could this be the Lord's hand, working all things together for good for those who love Him, and turning what some had meant for evil into good?[31] I requested the major give me a few days to see what the outcome of the National Guard's decision would be. He agreed.

Within a few days, I received my promotion orders from the Alabama National Guard to E-7, Sergeant First Class, but unsurprisingly there was a condition. I would have to drill in Centreville, Alabama because that was where the slot was located. I advised my company unit administrators in the Alabama National Guard that I had no intention of driving to Centreville for drills. They had improperly selected another soldier for the local slot in Eutaw for which I should have been considered, and I wanted to continue to drill in Eutaw. Perhaps the other soldier could drill in Centreville? It just seemed so wrong to me that they clearly had made a mistake and that in supposedly making it right, I would be further inconvenienced for the rest of my career. As expected, the administrators refused to place me in a slot at the Eutaw Alabama National Guard Armory. I thanked them kindly for the promotion and resigned my service with the Alabama National Guard.

Immediately, I called the major and informed him of my decision. He sent me the required paperwork for me to rejoin the United States Army Reserve. I traveled to Montgomery, Alabama, and completed the paperwork there. When I quickly became eligible for promotion, I was recommended to the promotion board and was promoted to E-8 master sergeant. As master sergeant, I was the non-commissioned officer in charge (NCOIC) of training, especially in field exercises. I reviewed various scenarios and responses to keep my team and our fellow Americans safe. We practiced performing missions, drilling one weekend a month and an additional two to three weeks every year. I remained with the U.S. Army Reserve for five years, until finally retiring from military service.

Thankfully, the Lord had not forgotten me in my struggle, and He had rewarded me for all my years of hard work and my tenacity in fighting for what was right. As a result of my actions, the local Alabama National Guard Unit was forced to discontinue its "good old boy" practices. Previously, the unit commander and the administrator picked their friends, or whatever individuals they wanted to promote, and recommended them to the promotion board without regard for qualified competition. This practice often kept Black soldiers from being moved up the ranks, despite their qualifications. Through my efforts and escalation of my concerns to my U.S. senator and representative, I had shone light upon their shady practices. Even though I did not receive the result I had wanted for myself within the National Guard, from then on, *all* soldiers, including African American soldiers, who qualified for promotion would go before the promotion board, thereby allowing the board to pick the best qualified soldier regardless of race. Also, I was pleased that the U.S. Army Reserve recognized my abilities and tenure and that they had appropriately promoted me.

Chapter 10

WAHSI

Throughout this period, I continued my community involvement. My respect for and work with the Freemasons had featured strongly throughout my adult life. In 1991, I received my thirty-second masonic degree and became a member of the Abraham Consistory #257 Ancient Accepted Scottish Rite in Demopolis, Alabama.

In addition, I served on the Board of Directors of the West Alabama Health Service, Inc. (WAHSI). In 1992, the Director of the organization submitted my name to the Board as a candidate for Board Chairman of WAHSI, and the Board approved. West Alabama Health Service, Inc. served as one of our nation's private, nonprofit, federally qualified health centers as authorized under Section 330 of the Public Health Service (PHS) Act to provide services to underserved populations. Such nonprofits serve 20% of rural residents' healthcare needs in the United States.[32] Organizations such as WAHSI which run outpatient clinics act as a much-needed safety net for poorer members of our communities. By complying with all health center program requirements, non-profit health centers like WAHSI qualify for reimbursement under Medicare and Medicaid. Health providers associated with WAHSI provided healthcare for our local and wider communities in Greene, Marengo, Hale, Choctaw, and Sumter Counties. The WAHSI Board of Directors reviewed and voted on policies and procedures we deemed appropriate for WAHSI. We also oversaw the functions and daily activities of the organization. WAHSI functioned as a financially stable, majority Black operated healthcare service, proudly meeting the needs of our community. I felt proud to be a part of WAHSI's mission.

With federal grants and reimbursements, we cared for the infirm and encouraged members of these local communities to seek preventative care, and thereby improved health outcomes in our area. We taught people how to care for themselves and held special classes for diabetics so they would understand how to eat properly for their condition and how to test their blood sugar levels and appropriately medicate themselves.[33] Additionally, beginning in Greene County, we provided our communities with onsite pharmacies which could meet their medication needs. Patients were charged for pharmaceuticals on a sliding scale. If patients lacked income to afford medications, we were able to provide them for free to our clients. We expanded pharmacy services to other counties in our territory as well.[34]

We observed a need for preventative dental care and other dental services. Therefore, we provided residents in our service area with access to affordable dentists and dental hygienists. Since Alabama state law disallowed nonprofits from hiring dentists, WAHSI opened the Eutaw Medical Clinic and another clinic in Mobile, Alabama to meet dental and other medical needs while complying with state law.[35] WAHSI also recognized a need for transportation services for many of our patients. We procured Medicaid funding to assist those in need with transportation to and from their doctors' offices, even picking them up at their front doors, when necessary.

In addition, WAHSI opened a youth clinic. We provided youth with physical examinations both for prevention and for school sports. We also taught youth about self-care, preventative care, and body awareness. We focused on teaching the participating youth in our communities about preventing both unwanted pregnancies and sexually transmitted diseases. We provided them with dental care and dental hygiene appointments. With close partnerships with Head Start programs and the local Boards of Education, we taught our youth about mental health, too. They learned that seeking mental health care was something to be encouraged, not ashamed of, and did not mean that one was "crazy." We were able to employ some of our youth during summers, giving them vital job experience, and during the school year, we employed AmeriCorps interns. Also, through additional grants, we were able to introduce our youth to the wider culture and were able to provide them with opportunities to travel out of state. On one field trip for which we had raised funds, we took our youth to the World Fair in Tennessee. Our students stayed in Knoxville College dormitories. Through experiences like these, our youth learned much about the wider world beyond their small towns and counties. Some had never left their home county before then. Many of these young people fell in love with the medical arts and sciences and pursued education and employment in the medical fields. [36]

We had succeeded in making our clinics one stop sites for nutrition training, medical care, self-care training, and pharmacy needs. We expanded our offerings to provide ambulance services for rural Greene County and hired RNs to ride along in ambulances to help monitor patients during the 35-minute drive to the hospital in Tuscaloosa. James Coleman, WAHSI's CEO for several years, was also concerned about the long drive to Tuscaloosa that women faced to see an obstetrician-gynecologist. Therefore, we brought an OB-GYN to our local Greene County hospital. This was no easy feat since insurance costs for OB-GYNs were high. We even contracted with a physician exchange service from overseas and worked with doctors who had loan obligations to bring talent to what might otherwise be deemed less exciting medical assignments. Doctors could work in low-income areas and work off their medical loans, so these arrangements were usually a win-win for both the doctors involved and our communities.[37]

The secret to WAHSI's success was our sincere commitment to our community and our desire to meet their needs above all else. Our staff diligently filed our Medicare and Medicaid claims both properly and in a timely manner so there would be minimal delay in reimbursements. Through constant grant writing, and demonstration of positive outcomes, we had raised millions of dollars in grant funding over the years to benefit deserving people in our communities. WAHSI was committed to keeping overhead as low as possible, including keeping staff expenses low. We funneled as much money as possible into service to others.

I served as Chairman until just before the organization dissolved in a court dispute after merging with another organization. The WAHSI administrator suggested to the Board of Directors that WAHSI should merge with a financially distressed majority white healthcare provider. He reasoned that we would not be in competition with them, and a merger could only strengthen our own healthcare facility. I had opposed the merger, fearing that the two healthcare organizations had vastly different agendas and that the other healthcare entity's clandestine interest was in taking over WAHSI services, but I was in the minority. Together, we became West Alabama Health Services, doing business as (DBA) Family Health Care. The relationship between the two healthcare providers was never good. Our two organizations soon became mired in disputes over claim processing. We soon learned that the organization with which we had merged had much higher overhead for their administrative staff, had little left over of their Section 330 funds for services to the community, and provided a more limited level of preventative care such as flu shots.[38] They failed to file their Medicare and Medicaid claims in a proper or timely manner.[39] Our staff was forced to jump in to help them with their backlog.

When our director left, the director from the other health service provider with whom we had merged became the new director over the new conglomerate organization.[40] A white man, he appeared to me to lack the same level of commitment to our Black citizens overall well-being as we had. He also seemed jealous of our successes. Iris Sermon had been our head of purchasing. She was promoted to CEO during this difficult period of transition. A gentleman from the regional office in Atlanta, Georgia, overseeing federally qualified health centers, intervened at that point. That new director and board falsely informed the government agency that our WAHSI team which I, as Board Chair, had overseen for years had not handled our records correctly.[41] They had asked the government to come in and "assist" us. Under this government oversight, the government official instructed both of the newly merged healthcare providers to dissolve their separate boards.[42] Accordingly, Iris Sermon dissolved our original WAHSI Board of Directors. All board members of our WAHSI team duly handed in their resignations, believing that the newly merged organization would have a completely new board of directors. However, the other board members of the health service group with whom we had merged did not resign as we had supposed. Thus, the other director and board secured a take-over.[43] They insisted we were "sitting on money" and instructed Ms. Sermon to require staff to work weekends to complete all billings. Amidst allegations that our WAHSI had misused funds, the district attorney's office from Birmingham arrived in our offices to search our computers and comb through our records. They required Ms. Sermon to lock up the organization and shut our doors.[44] However, the DA's office found nothing for which to indict us because we had run an exemplary organization.

Unable under the new leadership to pay our previous employees' last paychecks or unused vacation, we wound up in a bankruptcy court in Tuscaloosa, Alabama.[45] With the assistance of an attorney, Iris Sermon was finally able to provide final pay for lower and mid-level employees. However, our physicians and Ms. Sermon never received the funds due them.[46] Justice had not prevailed. After a lengthy court battle, the healthcare facility with which we merged was officially the owner of both our healthcare organizations. Once the union dissolved, the prevailing board kept the clinics they wanted but dismantled several others. Many people in our communities were unable to receive medical care or care to the level we had previously provided.[47] The new and unimproved WAHSI did not seem interested in providing quality services to the community. They appeared more interested in charging people than providing for people. They set up a unit out of state from where they could collect processing fees. I believe the court action caused economic hardship to the communities WAHSI had served under our leadership before the merger.

Chapter 11

EEOC Complaint Against the Local FSA

After many years of hard work and repeated attempts at different schools necessitated by job changes and relocations, I completed my Bachelor of Arts in Business Administration at Stillman College in May 1994.[48] This accomplishment fulfilled a lifelong dream. Daddy had highly valued education and his dying wish for me as a boy was for me to complete mine. What would Daddy have thought if he could have lived to see me graduate from college? I hoped my father was looking down from Heaven with pride for me. And I hoped Mama Carrie was pleased with me also. Just as she had taught me when fishing, I stayed with the challenge and never gave up despite the difficulties.

In lieu of a senior thesis, I prepared and submitted a Small Business Innovation Research (SBIR) grant proposal to the United States Department of Agriculture for Hall's Homemade Syrup. Although my sister Carrie Hall Gandy did not farm, she had excellent business sense. I approached her regarding working with me on the grant as a principal investigator, while I acted as project director, and she agreed.[49] Together we were a minority and half female run project team. We also consulted closely with Lucious Rodgers from the Tuskegee University Cooperative Extension Service and with "researchers from the Tuskegee University School of Agriculture and Home Economics."[50] Our objective was to standardize the quality of Hall's homemade ribbon cane and sorghum syrups. We wanted to take our homemade syrup from hobby to commercial enterprise. Our Phase I grant proposal received USDA funding. With grant funding, we modernized our operations and purchased equipment enabling us to improve quality and double output.[51] We also hired additional labor and purchased ribbon cane and sorghum juices from other local farmers.[52] As a result of our success with the grant proposal and our improvements in syrup manufacturing, I received the L. A. Potts Success Story Award, entitled "The Sweet Taste of Success" at the 52nd Annual Professional Agricultural Workers Conference at Tuskegee University in December 1994.[53]

As I finished the requirements for my B.A. in the spring of 1994, heavy rains continued to fall.[54] Farmers in the surrounding areas of Alabama near me faced difficulties planting crops early enough in the season because of the wet conditions and then in maintaining crops once they were planted. The roots of plants became waterlogged in flooded fields, and the grasses competed with crops and overran them as the wet conditions kept us out of the fields. Farmers in much of the South including Greene County, Alabama were unable to follow normal cultivation practices. Wet weather challenged farmers' normal application of fertilizer and herbicide that year since fertilizer and herbicide would be washed away.[55] And yet, I cared for my fields appropriately, cultivating and fertilizing when I could. Besides policing, farming remained my passion.

The USDA recognized many areas in the South in 1994 as suffering agricultural disaster and approved disaster relief payments for affected farmers. On February 7, 1995, I filed several applications to the USDA to request disaster relief payments to cover the losses I had suffered on crops on my farms.[56] The U.S. Agriculture Consolidated Farm Service Agency (FSA) Committee, Greene County, Alabama Office convened on March 14, 1995 to review my application.[57] They concluded that I had not followed acceptable farming practices for several crops in my various fields and therefore denied me any disaster relief.[58] I was stunned. I had been farming in Greene County most of my life. My family had farmed here before me. All these years, I had worked closely with the Cooperative Extension Services through Tuskegee and Auburn Universities. I had won awards for my farming practices.[59] I had been awarded a grant for one of my farming operations.[60] On what basis could they justify a claim that I did not follow acceptable farming practices? What could I possibly have done differently than I had during that disastrous 1994 growing season?

I filed for an appeal. The Greene County FSA Committee, comprised of Joe McGee, Willice Lashley, and L. C. Bambarger, scheduled the appeal hearing for April 18, 1995.[61] [62] I sat before an all-white, male committee and one elderly nonvoting male minority member. None of the Committee members represented small scale minority farming.[63] I sat as the committee members had the audacity to tell me to my face that I had not followed acceptable farming practices; as they claimed I did not apply herbicides or fertilizers; as they stated that I should not grow my own plants or use my own seed from previous harvests; as they insisted the monetary amounts I claimed I had lost on various crops were too high. I listened in a dizzying mixture of disbelief, hurt, and anger. This felt personal.

I countered all their false allegations. I indicated I had receipts to show my fertilizer purchases. I pointed out that, regardless, the county had been declared an agricultural disaster area because of the wet conditions which prevented us from cultivating as usual. I showed them data from Auburn and Tuskegee Universities which indicated a farmer should grow their own seedlings for planting and save their own seed from the previous harvest. It was true that the monetary amount I claimed per acre for fruits and vegetables exceeded what farmers planting row crops like soy, corn or cotton claimed per acre in damages. However, fruits and vegetables are high-volume crops and are labor intensive. They produce more monetary value per acre than do row crops which can be harvested by machine. On the other hand, they cost more to produce due to the labor costs. Therefore, the loss on such crops is greater. None of these are difficult concepts. I do not believe they understood how Black farmers in general needed to farm differently because their farms tended to be smaller—only 10-12 acres, usually, and up to 40 acres at most— so they often plant higher volume fruit and vegetable crops. Or perhaps they just did not care. But I knew farming and was an expert in small-scale farming for profit. To bolster my claims, I showed them the research data from Tuskegee University stating how much income could be generated from one acre of high-volume crops.

The FSA Committee looked at the research data I presented from Auburn and Tuskegee Universities' Extension Service offices and ignored it or flat out denied the factual data in front of their eyes. Despite having no defense for denying my disaster relief claims, they informed me I needed to visit other farms to see how farming should be practiced. I replied I had been farming for an extensive length of time, most of my life, in fact. I had attended many farming workshops sponsored by both Auburn and Tuskegee Universities, and I was well-versed in small scale farming. Perhaps most astounding and galling of all was the white male Auburn University extension agent who sided with the FSA Committee. He, of all people, should have known better. I had expected more from him, and I had had a right to.

We had reached an impasse. They remained resolute in their denial of my disaster relief application. We took a break. It had become clear to me that what they took umbrage with was not factual data but with a successful Black farmer and sheriff who would not genuflect before white society. I could not believe that the FSA Committee similarly treated other farmers seeking disaster relief in Greene County. Surely, the committee had not scrutinized other farmers utilizing less scientifically sound farming methods as they had scrutinized me. I suspected, as well, that this was an opportunity for them to retaliate against me for previous refusals to submit to their racial discrimination and for my bankruptcy claim which had denied them the opportunity to foreclose on my property. I could think of no other logical explanations for their stubborn resistance to documented facts.

I informed Richard Burge, the FSA District Director over Greene County, who had also attended, that I would appeal their decision to the Alabama State FSA Committee office and file a complaint against the Greene County Farm Service Agency for racial discrimination. The next day, I spoke with Auburn University's Greene County extension service agent from the night before. I told him I felt he and the FSA Committee had treated me unfairly. He informed me that after I left, the Committee had reconsidered their previous determination and might possibly reduce my yield payment instead of outright denying my claims.[64]

I believe the FSA Committee changed their determination regarding my disaster relief payments to appease me and to dissuade me from appealing their decision to the Alabama State Farm Service Agency Committee or reporting them for discrimination, and also to improve their position and image if I did follow through with my promised action against them.[65] I suppose they thought I would be grateful that they awarded me anything after originally denying me completely and that I would back down. Their behavior, however, was wrong. If they were treating me this way, I suspected other Black farmers may have been facing similar discriminatory actions throughout Alabama and the South. I knew that most Black farmers were ill-equipped to formally complain because they may not have known how to go about filing those very complaints, routinely receiving less agency support than white farmers in many places. They may not have known they even qualified for benefits or known they had recourse when they were treated unfairly. They also may have lacked an income independent from farming as I had through my role as sheriff. Many Black folks felt it was a no-win situation to fight a government agency. It was not without cause that the USDA was called "The Last Plantation" in the Black community. I was presented with this challenge, and I felt a duty to fight for what was right, not just for myself but for others to have their full rights as citizens of the United States. Sometimes, God taps you on the shoulder and whispers into your heart to stand, and then you must stand, even when it is difficult, even when it costs you.

On April 20, 1995, I formally appealed their decision to the State of Alabama Farm Service Agency office. In addition, I filed a formal complaint with David Montoya, Director of the USDA Office of Civil Rights Enforcement in Washington, D.C. for possible racial discrimination and requested an investigation, determination, and appropriate corrective action should they determine my allegations well-founded.[66]

With a quick turnaround, on May 5, 1995, the State FSA Committee reversed the Greene County FSA Committee actions.[67] Richard Burge had noted in his memorandum that Daniel Robinson, STO Chief Program Specialist, Production Adjustment, found the county committee's decision to deny benefits to me based on using the past year's seed invalid because saving seed is a common and approved practice.[68] The State Committee agreed I should receive the original monetary request for disaster relief for which I had applied. They had found no merit in the Greene County FSA Committee's initial disapproval of my application for disaster relief or their subsequent payment yield reductions.[69] Thanks to their quick review, I then promptly received the full disaster relief payments. Now I would need to wait on the USDA Office of Civil Rights Enforcement to investigate and decide whether the local FSA Committee's actions were due to racial discrimination.

While relations with the FSA had been less than ideal since the early days of our relationship, the situation went from bad to worse and tensions escalated between the USDA, FSA and me. The Greene County FSA Committee members along with their associates in the white community blackballed me, and their actions were a source of significant hardship for me. The local farm co-op and co-ops of surrounding counties refused me credit. Local white farmers refused to sell me hay. I had previously assisted one of the white farmers by taking my tractor to his farm and rolling hay for him. Now he refused to sell me even one roll of hay. To purchase hay, I had to travel to adjacent Tuscaloosa

County where no one knew my situation. If they had known, they most likely would not have sold to me either.

The white community did not find enough satisfaction in blackballing me from local and surrounding white-owned establishments. They also decided to wreak emotional devastation upon me by turning the Black community against me. Certain members of the white community lied about me to local Blacks with whom they had contact and pressured and threatened them into ostracizing me. Some in the Black community approached me early in this period to caution me that the white folks in Greene County were conspiring to undermine me. Then Black friends informed me that they had to stop associating with me or they would lose their standing with their white "friends." One friend with whom I had hoped to work a deal for some top-quality beef cattle through the Heifer International Project cut all ties with me because of the pressure upon him to dissociate himself from me. Some in the Black farming community who needed to request loans from the banks were informed they needed to cease all

friendship with me, or they would receive no financial assistance from the local banks. They stirred up animosity between me and the Black community in the political arena as well. People began telling me that I did not need to own and operate a farm while being sheriff. Ironically, at no point had people indicated they saw a problem with the previous sheriff who was a white man who had also owned a farm. Few stood by me through this. I was thankful that Donald and Harry Means, who were more financially independent than most, had not turned their backs on me as others had. I tried to explain to these other farmers what was happening and my need for them to stand with me in my fight, but most did not want to associate with me out of fear of reprisal.

On October 2, 1995, John W. Dumas, District Director from Forsyth, Georgia completed his review of my allegation of racial discrimination and submitted a thorough and detailed report of the Greene County FSA Committee's actions against me to Ms. Barbara Nelson of the Equal Employment Opportunity and Civil Rights Staff.[70] Dumas had reviewed both the state and local FSA committees' minutes and records.[71] He also spoke with other experts regarding best farming practices. He found that my saving seed from previous harvests and using them in my planting was a common practice.[72] He found that there was no indication that any of the other 1994 disaster applicants had been questioned regarding their use of fertilizer or herbicides or that the use of such chemicals had factored into their decision to approve disaster benefits applications.[73] Neither had they reduced any other disaster applicants' payments as they had mine.[74] Dumas noted that Daniel Robinson, the USDA specialist, had found nothing in my records that warranted either the initial disapprovals or subsequent payment yield reductions.[75] Now my case would need to be investigated further to determine if the Greene County FSA Committee's actions were racially motivated.

With all the blowback I experienced locally for taking a stand against injustice, I was very thankful for honest people within the U.S. government like John Dumas and the specialists who had weighed in on the validity of my farming practices. Dumas wrote a thorough report detailing the discrepancies between the county FSA's standards for and treatment of me versus those they employed for other farmers. He had validated all my claims and suspicions. Unfortunately, his findings did not ease the pressure upon me in my community.

Chapter 12

Racial Tensions Mounting

I was hardly the only one who continued to face racial prejudice and discrimination in 1996. Racial tensions were high throughout the South and within Greene County, Alabama. On Friday, December 22, 1995, the Mt. Zion Baptist church on the outskirts of Boligee, in Greene County, Alabama, was burned to the ground. Three weeks later, on Thursday, January 11, 1996, Mt. Zoar Baptist and Little Zion Baptist churches, both within a six-mile radius of Boligee, were also burned down.[76] Three catastrophic fires at African American churches within a six-mile radius of Boligee within such a short timeframe—two in the same night, no less—roused suspicions of arson, both locally and federally. A rash of arson fires against churches and synagogues during the 1990s had captured the attention of the Bureau of Alcohol, Tobacco, Firearms and Explosives (ATF) and Federal Bureau of Investigations (FBI). While arsonists also targeted predominately white churches and during this period, a disproportionately large number of churches they burned down were owned by African Americans.

The ATF traveled to Boligee, Alabama on January 13, 1996, to investigate the church fires because they had noticed similarities to five recent arson fires in Tennessee against one interracial and four Black churches. They suspected arson in the Boligee church fires as well.[77] The Sheriff's Office and I worked with State of Alabama investigators, the ATF, and the FBI. Initially, these agencies bypassed me, instead beginning their investigations by speaking with the white mayor of Boligee, A. L. "Buddy" Lavender. Mayor Lavender was acting as both police and fire chiefs of Boligee at the time.[78] However, the church arson fires had occurred outside his jurisdiction. Furthermore, arson, as a felony, rightfully fell under the jurisdiction of the sheriff's office, not the town's jurisdiction. I informed these federal agents that their actions were improper and set them straight on lines of authority within Greene County. Moving forward they would need to consult with my office and me. It vexed me that I had to confront them in this manner. Here they were investigating possible hate crimes in the form of arson against African Americans in the Boligee area, and they had failed to recognize me as the lead law enforcement official in the county. I assigned a deputy from the sheriff's office to work and coordinate with federal investigators.

The FBI never revealed their findings in the arson investigations to my office, and I do not know if they ever found the culprits. There was no resolution; no one was prosecuted. A part of me has long entertained the idea that even if the ATF and the FBI had found suspects in the arson fires, they may have been reluctant to identify those involved for fear of inciting an uproar within the predominantly African American community in Greene County. Perhaps they hoped with the passing of time and the rebuilding of the three African American churches, the racial unrest in the county would die down.

The extreme racial divide in Greene County, Alabama still remained in 1996. The county population was 82% African American.[79] Within the town limits of Eutaw and Boligee, the populations were predominantly white, and consequently the mayors of Eutaw and Boligee were both white. Most, though not all, of the county officials in 1996 were African American, reflecting the racial composition of those voting districts.[80] This was a significant improvement from prior to the civil rights movement of the 1950s and 1960s and the Voting Rights Act of 1965, when African Americans had been disenfranchised and only whites held political power in Alabama. Nonetheless, Greene County, the smallest and poorest county in Alabama, remained extremely racially divided.[81] Blacks and whites still had separate banks, separate newspapers, separate swimming pools, and separate churches with exception of a small racially integrated Catholic church.[82] The country club members were all white. The public school was nearly all Black with the remainder of the school population comprised of other minorities while the local private school was all white. Even in our local restaurants, Blacks and whites sat in separate areas, no longer by law but by social custom.[83] In Greene County, Alabama in the 1990s, Blacks and whites had little contact conducive to developing any real and lasting friendships.

After the arson fires, white volunteers from churches, synagogues, and other volunteer groups flocked to our county to help rebuild our churches. These volunteers worked side by side with African American community members and these white volunteers attended our Black churches on Sundays, worshiping side by side with us. A few white members of our community also crossed the racial divide to work with Blacks in rebuilding.[84] These evil acts of arson could have been the impetus for real healing and reconciliation in our community and for a renewed opportunity at racial integration, but unfortunately, that healing did not occur, and Greene remained as divided and racially tense afterwards as before.

The Alabama Advisory Committee to the United States Commission on Civil Rights (AACUSCCR) held a hearing on July 2, 1996, in Boligee to ascertain the nature of and to improve race relations in our communities. As much as things had changed from our protests in the 1960s, things still remained the same. Some in the community refused to believe that there were any racial tensions in Greene County, claiming openly there were no problems between Blacks and whites.[85] Such people had also believed there were no problems between Blacks and whites when Blacks were unable to vote in Alabama and when Blacks had to step off sidewalks to make way for whites and avoid eye contact, lest there be repercussions. As a community leader, I spoke at that first hearing and expressed my concerns over race relations. Based on my experience living and working in Alabama most of my life, the only thing that had changed regarding race relations was the outward appearances. Behaviors had changed as dictated by law, but if one were to scratch beneath the surface of Southern society, the attitudes that had driven racist behavior in the past were still there. Conditions had certainly improved. There were no separate facilities in buildings for Blacks and whites, for example. However, there remained an undercurrent of racism and unrest. I witnessed and personally experienced many whites still trying to get away with whatever they could.

Over the course of a year, other community leaders and I tried to bring whites and Blacks together to discuss possible methods to bridge the gap between us. On June 26, 1997, the AACUSCCR returned to Boligee to assess our progress in racial reconciliation. They requested I speak to the panel at that public hearing as well. I informed them that although we had tried to move forward, we still had a race problem, despite the position of some leaders in the community that there were no Black-White issues. I expressed my concerns for Greene County, saying that we would all perish together as a community if we did not find a way to work with a common purpose towards common goals. I expressed my opinion that Blacks were very willing to work with whites, but in my experience the white community objected to any Black equality or leadership. As I had observed, whites were fine with working with Blacks so long as whites were in charge and Blacks followed.[86] I explained that I thought some white folks may have feared retaliation from Blacks for years of mistreatment. Yet a desire for revenge was far from the prevailing attitude among the Black citizenry. I asserted, by way of example, that as sheriff I had treated Blacks and whites equally, never abusing my authority.[87] My integrity dictated that I treat both Blacks and whites with dignity and respect.

It bothered me that my county suffered due to racial discord. During the forums hosted by the AACUSCCR, I explained how whites would recognize elected white officials publicly by their titles. However, when whites met me on the street, they simply addressed me as "George." Other African American leaders in the community also faced this sort of disrespect. Had this familiarity been equally applied, it would not have been problematic, yet it was not. Another thing I found hurtful at that second AACUSCCR hearing was the insinuation by some that there were not really any Black-white issues, but that there was a serious Black-Black problem, a classic way to deflect the conversation away from interracial problems.[88] I testified that there was no Black-Black problem any more than there was a white-white problem.[89] Throughout the country, most crime is committed against others of the same race; this is not specifically an African-

American problem. The forums allowed the community to voice their concerns, but they offered little by way of substance to change the race relations situation in Greene County.

Chapter 13

Vindication Against the Local FSA

In the interim, on August 6, 1996, ten months after Dumas revealed his findings in his investigation of my complaint regarding denial of my disaster relief benefits for questionable reasons, the USDA's Center for Civil Rights Operations issued its program complaint final decision. After a thorough investigation, they found discrimination against me on the basis of race.[90] As I reviewed their findings, I learned that the State Chief Program Specialist had contacted the District Director on April 14, 1995 in advance of the appeals hearing with the Greene County FSA Committee which was held on April 18, 1995, informing him that the county committee had improperly denied my disaster relief applications based on the use of prior year's seeds for peanuts and potatoes.[91] He had apparently implied that District Director Richard Burge should attend the April 18 appeal hearing to monitor the proceedings.[92] His presence now made sense. Also, after arguing vehemently with me over the improper use of prior year's seed, the County Committee, having been alerted to their error, stated that their continued denial of my benefits claim was not for use of prior year's seed (as they had claimed in their initial denial) but for supposed insufficient use of herbicide and pesticide.[93] Even when they knew they were wrong, they had trumped up a means of proceeding in their actions against me!

The USDA Civil Rights Operations investigators found clear evidence that I had been treated differently than all white farmers in our community in similar situations.[94] The Greene County FSA Committee had applied different standards to me specifically. All other applications were approved expeditiously while mine was singled out for denial.[95] No other applicant had been questioned regarding whether he had used conventional or unconventional farming methods. Wet weather had prevented all of us from cultivating and harvesting our crops as we normally would have, but I was the only one questioned or rejected for so-called unconventional farming practices.

The investigators had also noted that there had been recent vandalism of local Black churches and that when a Black judge had sentenced two white men to prison for the vandalism, someone shot at his home with multiple shotgun blasts.[96] They deemed our area as racially hostile. In addition, an unnamed member of the local FSA Committee had suggested that my outside income should be used to offset my crop losses even though this was not a legitimate reason to deny a disaster relief claim. He, however, did not argue that white farmers should similarly use their incomes from outside jobs.[97] He also openly referred to a Black county commissioner as a "boy,"[98] a manner in which Southern white men have degraded Black men for centuries, indicating their supposed inferiority to whites as though they could not attain full-fledged adult status. He also had remarked to others that the Black community was a "baby factory" and said Black people are irresponsible and bad with money.[99] Based on their detailed analysis, the Greene County Farm Service Agency had clearly discriminated against me because of my race.

Because the State FSA had quickly reversed the County's denial of disaster relief benefits and had given me the full amount to which I was entitled like other farmers in my area, there were no additional monetary disbursements. However, they did insist on corrective action aimed at ensuring this kind of discrimination would not recur in the county.[100] Although they had been elected to the FSA Committee by the local farming community, on August 22, 1996, the USDA removed Joe McGee and Willice Lashley from their positions on the Farm Service Agency Committee, pending appeal.[101] Their removal was permanent, and they were disallowed from ever being reinstated to any other USDA committee.[102] They were replaced on the committee with two alternates, Fred H. Hughes and Harry Means, both local Black men, who would represent Greene County on the newly combined Greene/Sumter FSA. This was a historic event for our community. Hughes and Means were the first African Americans to serve on the Greene County FSA Committee.[103] There was no local memory of anyone having been removed from our FSA Committee before; this underscored the level of proof the USDA Civil Rights Operations investigators had accumulated and the seriousness of their behavior.[104] Hughes and Means finished out McGee's and Lashley's terms. They served well, attempting to do right by the farmers in the community, regardless of their race. I could not have been more pleased.

In 1996, during this discrimination investigation and the arson fire investigations, my agricultural endeavors continued to ground me and provide me with relief from outside pressures. I continued working on improving the production of Hall's Homemade Syrup. While working on Part II of Phase I of the USDA Small Business Innovation Research (SBIR) grant, I applied for Phase II in 1996. The objective in Phase II was to commercialize the syrup and other products which used the syrup as a base, e.g., as a sugar substitute and as a sweetener in drinks and candies. Our Hall's Homemade Syrup operation would need to acquire a million-dollar loan to build additional facilities, to purchase additional equipment, and for start-up funds to implement mass production in Phase II. Again, the USDA approved us for the SBIR grant. We had hoped to avail our business enterprise of funds available through the Empowerment Zones and Enterprise Communities Act of 1993 and other Alabama State agencies and programs available in our area. The $1,000,000 loan we sought would have been backed by the federal government. However, we still needed to receive approval through local white banking and FSA personnel. I believe those loans were denied in retaliation for my work as sheriff, my bankruptcy in lieu of the foreclosure and auctioning off of my property, and my formal complaints of racial discrimination against the U.S. Agriculture Consolidated Farm Service Agency Committee in Greene County.

Chapter 14

Community Backlash

Concurrently, a certain reporter for the Greene County Independent, a local newspaper, began spinning news articles which I felt defamed my character and the sheriff's office with exaggerations and distortions of fact. They printed articles with titles such as "Absentee Sheriff." I believe they acted in retaliation because I would not allow reporters from this local newspaper to have access to incident reports that were under investigation. The publisher wanted the paper's reporters to come to the sheriff's office on Monday mornings and comb through the weekend activity reports. They habitually plastered news stories of local Blacks arrested across their pages but seldomly printed articles on local white criminal activity or misdemeanors. The racism that underlies this sort of behavior was unacceptable to me, and I refused them access to our files. The paper's publisher sidestepped me and scurried to the Attorney General to get their way. Again, I stood my ground for what I believed was right and in turn asked the Attorney General for an opinion. The Attorney General ruled that I did not have to allow them access to reports under investigation if this was the policy of our department, which in fact it was.

Needless to say, the Greene County Independent was no fan of mine. They proceeded to publish articles complaining about the $50,000 annual salary I received as sheriff, as though this were unusual. They falsely implied to the State of Alabama Department of Public Health that Hall's Homemade Syrup operation did not adequately adhere to health standards. They complained about me to the State of Alabama Department of Revenue. Both the Alabama Department of Public Health and the Alabama Department of Revenue investigated their claims. After thorough reviews, the Alabama Department of Revenue found nothing improper, and the Alabama Department of Public Health merely directed me to insert covers over light bulbs in the building in case they were to break. They found the newspaper's allegations to be false.

Around the same time, I filed as a lead plaintiff in a major lawsuit, and as expected, there was blowback in the community over the stand I took. Some in the community stirred up local Black church leaders against me as well by insinuating that I did not perform my duties as sheriff properly because I had an additional job on my farm. Soon Black church leaders were quoted in the local paper as saying, "You cannot find the Sheriff because he is moored up in syrup." While some may have believed these negative assertions about me, there is a long and hurtful history of a small number of Blacks working with whites against their own community. Doing so, they have believed, has given them status and clout within the white community. The attacks continued over a period of three years until I was voted out of office in 1999.

Being voted out as sheriff hurt me deeply, down to the depths of my soul. My heart felt heavy because my own people seemed to believe the slanderous slurs against me and failed to see how I was trying to bring justice and fairness to the community. Being a Black sheriff in Greene County was particularly challenging. My goal always had been nothing less than to help the community, protecting them from racial discrimination, the best I could, and to ensure equal justice for all. I knew that some Black citizens felt I should have been more lenient toward them because I too was Black and should understand their plight. On the other hand, some white citizens felt I should have been more lenient toward them because they were white and therefore should be privileged. I, however, had endeavored to treat both Blacks and whites equally and fairly under the law. As a man of faith, it was my belief in the Lord and my knowledge of the Scriptures that helped me through this dark time in my life. The great Prophet Moses had led the children of Israel out of slavery in Egypt. The whole time he advocated for them before Pharaoh, the people complained. As he led them out of Egypt and into the desert towards the Promised Land, they complained. If someone as great as Moses who followed the Lord so closely, who spoke face to face with God, and who did so much to help his people received so much flack, then how could I expect I would be exempt from this sort of suffering? This line of reasoning did not eradicate the hurt, but it did help put it in perspective. The Lord was my comfort. Sometimes, it seemed, He was the only one on my side.

Chapter 15

Pigford v. Glickman

From early 1982 through August 1997, I had spent many restless nights studying USDA rules and regulations and addressing correspondence to and responding to correspondence from the local, state, and national FSA offices. I also spent innumerable hours attending hearing after hearing, appeal after appeal, and mediation meeting after mediation meeting. I am certain white farmers did not need to expend this level of energy on understanding the workings and regulations of the USDA. Many of the problems I suffered with the county FSA were holdovers from my purchase of farmland with the former FmHA with my home as collateral and my subsequent decision to file for bankruptcy. Representative Earl Hilliard's office had been instrumental in assisting me with my discrimination complaint against the National Guard and in finally receiving my promotion in 1993. I contacted him to alert him to the problems I experienced with the USDA and FSA as well.

Meanwhile, Representative Hilliard had heard complaints from other U.S. representatives from Mississippi and North Carolina regarding the USDA's treatment of Black farmers in their states. The cries against racially motivated loan reductions, delays, and denials, and of denying or reducing disaster relief on the basis of race had reached the halls of Congress. A staff member from Representative Hilliard's office contacted me for additional information regarding my own experiences in agriculture and with the USDA and its Farmer's Home Administration. Representative Hilliard also wished to know if I would be willing to testify in front of Congress regarding the discriminatory treatment I had received. Yes. Yes, I would.

In the interim, Sam E. Taylor, who was an agricultural specialist with the Washington, D.C. law firm Tuttle, Taylor, and Heron had been in contact with Rep. Hilliard and reached out to me. He had also connected with Timothy Pigford, a soybean and corn farmer from Cumberland County, North Carolina and Lloyd Shaffer, a soybean farmer from Jackson, Mississippi in the Mississippi Delta region. In 1976, Tim Pigford had applied for a loan to purchase a 175-acre farm on the outskirts of Wilmington, North Carolina.[105] The FmHA approved a loan to construct a home and later a loan for operating expenses for rented property.[106] However, they refused his loan application for purchase of land.[107] After several years, Tim Pigford complained of the mistreatment he had received, and in September 1984, he testified before Congress about his experiences with racism in farming.[108] Shortly thereafter, Pigford was denied eligibility for both operating and land ownership loans for 1985 due to his "lack of experience," despite having farmed and received operating loans for years.[109] Eventually the government foreclosed on the Pigford home.[110]

Lloyd Shaffer, whom Taylor had also contacted, had farmed as a hired hand on white-owned farms and assisted on relatives' farms since he was a teenager, so he had years of farming experience by the time he turned to the USDA's Farmer's Home Administration for a loan to purchase a 200-acre farm with a house.[111] The loan officer took his loan application and tossed it into the trash can right in front of him.[112] The following year, Shaffer leased a large farm so he could grow soybeans. His operating loan and equipment loans were denied. He appealed, and the operating loan was approved for half of what he needed, leaving him dependent on other farmers' equipment to plant and harvest. He was unable to plant until May and unable to harvest until December, so his yields were insufficient to earn him enough to pay off the loans.[113] After a few years of this repeating pattern of late loan approvals which led to low crop yields throughout the early to mid-1990s, the lending organization foreclosed upon him.[114]

Despite living in three different states, our experiences with the USDA through the FmHA were discouragingly similar. Our repeated complaints had done little to change the system or to improve our situations. Taylor suggested we hire attorneys to help us in our quest for justice. I contacted local attorneys from Selma, Tuscaloosa, and other cities in Alabama to inquire if they would represent me. However, they declined. My impression was that they did not want to sue the federal government due to the limited resources of their offices. Therefore, Taylor scheduled a meeting for us with an attorney in Washington, D.C., named Alex Pires of Conlon, Frantz, Phelan, Pires & Leavy, who was known for his work with farmers.

Early in our discussions with Taylor and Pires, we were scheduled to testify before Congress, but those plans were derailed. Tim Pigford, Lloyd Shaffer, and I had driven up to Washington, D.C. together. I remember walking to the Capitol building with them in advance of our scheduled appearance. I had thought about the weight of responsibility on us to represent our own experiences with the USDA and, by extension, those of many other Black farmers, to our nation's Congressional representatives. Apparently, however, shortly before we were scheduled to appear,

Justice Department attorney Michael Sitcov and Pires had met, and afterwards, Taylor informed Pigford, Shaffer, and me that we would not appear before Congress after all. It was unclear to us what conversations had taken place behind the scenes to stall the process. I was disappointed that I was unable to testify, especially since we had driven all that way. Surely, I thought, if Congress could only hear first-hand about our struggles and the racial discrimination we had faced from the USDA, they would act in the interest of African American citizens like us. After all, they had passed important laws to curtail racial discrimination. With a full Congressional investigation, I had believed they would uncover the depth of the racism in the USDA and had hoped they would set things right.

Under the advice of Pires, Tim Pigford, Lloyd Shaffer, and I filed a civil rights class action complaint on behalf of ourselves and similarly situated African American farmers against the United States Department of Agriculture in the United States District Court in Washington, D.C. on August 28, 1997. Pires had taken up the case and led the charge for justice. The lawsuit would be known as Pigford v. Glickman (1999) (Civil Action No. 97-1978) and would quickly become one of the largest lawsuits in the history of the United States. Because of the enormity of this case, Pires would work closely with another D.C. attorney named Phillip L. Fraas of Tuttle, Taylor & Heron. Fraas also had expertise in agricultural legal cases. Before long, six other law offices would also join the lawsuit. J. L. Chestnut of Chestnut, Sanders, Sanders, and Pettaway in Alabama were among those who stepped forward to assist at that point. Pires would remain my primary attorney, and I communicated primarily with him. However, I did occasionally interact with Fraas as well.

While a lawsuit was not my first choice, Pires was a talented attorney who could draw attention to the USDA's discriminatory practices which denied African Americans farm loans that would have been granted to white farmers, or reduced them, setting Black farmers up for failure. Bringing attention to the situation was crucial, especially now that it was clear how widespread these corrupt and racist practices were across the South. Black farmers were engaged in a life and death battle as they were ousted from their homes and denied their livelihoods. No one willing to work hard in the United States should be denied the right to make a living on account of their race. Hopefully with this lawsuit, we would achieve justice for ourselves and other Black farmers who, like us, had faced discrimination. If we successfully proved our case in this lawsuit—and I had no doubt we would as we had so much evidence—there would, of course, be some financial remuneration. However, the most important result would be creating a system of fairness for Black Americans to farm their land alongside white Americans so we could continue to provide food and other plant-based products for our country while earning our livings. Farming our own land should be our dream, not our nightmare. The light of truth would shine on the corruptness of the system and drive it out! Without us shedding light upon these illegal and unethical practices, the problems would never change.

In a sense, I felt called to do this work. As a police officer and a sheriff, I had considerable experience filing complaints and understood the importance of accurate and adequate documentation. Also, because of my previously substantiated complaints, I had all the proof I needed, proof that is so often lacking in these sorts of disputes. Therefore, I was better positioned to fight this battle than some others may have been. And I felt it was my duty to stand for truth and for those who may not be as equipped to fight the system, just as I had always done.

With the filing of Pigford v. Glickman, the other plaintiffs and I were catapulted into a battle of both personal turmoil and profound import, the likes of which we could not have imagined. Other plaintiffs joined our case. These included Eddie Ross from Warren County, Mississippi, and Lucious Abrams, of eastern Georgia.[115] Eddie Ross was the son and grandson of farmers and had farmed in some capacity nearly all his life. As a young man in his 20's, he worked on a 100-acre white owned farm and a 47-acre leased farm which he ran himself.[116] Several years later, he devised a plan to farm a nearly 800-acre farm with soybean and cotton. He had the know-how; he just needed the loan to lease the land. In 1991, he was denied the loan by the FmHA for "inadequate management ability/experience for scope of planned operation", even though he had farmed larger plots of land for years and all the white farmers' loans had been approved even for those still young in their late 20's like himself.[117] In May, the USDA overturned the county committee's decision after Ross appealed, and they acknowledged racial discrimination as the motivating factor in the original loan denial.[118] However, the funds were not released until June. Therefore, it was too late to plant cotton, and the beans, planted as late as they were, failed to produce an adequate harvest.[119] Ross faced the same predicament as so many of the rest of us had, a continuing cycle of late loan disbursals and the resultant poor harvests. He continued to file discrimination complaints, and he continued to face reprisals from the county committee for his filings. He had traveled back and forth to Washington, D.C. several times. Eventually, he was awarded

$500,000 as a settlement in early 1997. However, considering the Pigford v. Glickman class action lawsuit filed later that August, the USDA reneged. Adding insult to injury, the IRS sent him a document showing how much he owed in taxes on the nonexistent settlement payment.[120]

Lucious Abrams's story was similar to ours as well. He was a fourth-generation farmer on 2000-acres of land, but he faced the cycle of late loan payments, leading to late planting and harvesting and poor yields.[121] The discrimination he had faced propelled him to action, and he too became a plaintiff in Pigford v. Glickman.

Eventually, another farmer, Cecil Brewington, joined as a plaintiff in Pigford v. Glickman. Brewington had also filed a class action suit against the USDA for racial discrimination against African American farmers. On January 5, 1999, under the order from United States District Judge Paul L. Friedman, the Brewington, et al. v. Glickman, Civil Action No. 98-1693, was joined with the Pigford, et al. v. Glickman civil action complaint.[122] The now combined class action suit would cover:

> "All African American farmers who (1) farmed, or attempted to farm, between January 1, 1981 and December 31, 1996; (2) applied to the United States Department of Agriculture (USDA) during that time period for participation in a federal farm credit or benefit program and who believed that they were discriminated against on the basis of race in USDA's response to that application; and (3) filed a discrimination complaint on or before July 1, 1997, regarding USDA's treatment of such farm credit or benefit application."[123]

Additional provisions were made for those who had missed the cutoff date of July 1, 1997, extending the deadline to September 12, 2000. Later, due to concerns over the large number of late filings and complaints about insufficient representation, the 2008 farm bill would permit these additional claims to be consolidated into another class action case known as Pigford II. The application deadline for Pigford II was May 11, 2012.[124]

The court order also delineated two tracks claimants could follow in their pursuit of justice, as detailed below:

"A. Track A claims will be decided by a neutral adjudicator without an oral hearing, based solely on the claim package that the class member submits, along with any written materials submitted by USDA. Class members choosing track A would be required to show by "substantial evidence" that they experienced discrimination in a USDA credit or benefit program at any time between January 1, 1981 and December 31, 1996, that as a direct result of that discrimination they suffered economic damage, and that they had filed a complaint of discrimination with USDA between January 1, 1981 and July 1, 1997. "Substantial evidence" is a lower burden of proof than is required under Track B. Class members who prevail under the Track A process would receive: (1) discharge of all outstanding debt to USDA that is affected by the discriminatory conduct they experienced, (2) a cash payment of $50,000, and (3) an additional payment made directly to the Internal Revenue Service equal to 25% of the sum of the principal amount of debt forgiven and the $50,000 (this payment to the IRS would be used to help pay any tax liability occasioned by the award). B. Under Track B, class members' claims would be decided by an arbitrator after an oral hearing lasting not more than 8 hours, during which both the class member and USDA could present evidence. The class member would be required to demonstrate, by a "preponderance of the evidence" that he experienced discrimination in a USDA credit or benefit program at any time between January 1, 1981 and December 31, 1996, that as a direct result of that discrimination he suffered economic damage, and that he had filed a complaint of discrimination with USDA between January 1, 1981 and July 1, 1997. The preponderance of the evidence standard is a higher one than the "substantial evidence,' test that will apply to Track A claims. Class members who succeed on their claims under Track B would be entitled to a cash payment equal to their actual damages, and forgiveness of all of outstanding USDA loans that were affected by the discriminatory conduct. Track B is not available to class members who assert only non-credit benefit claims. Class members who do not prevail on a claim under Track A or Track B will receive no monetary or injunctive relief, and have no right to appeal the adverse decision."[125]

Being a plaintiff in the Pigford v. Glickman Black farmers' lawsuit proved to be one of the most daunting experiences I had ever encountered in my life. The other lead plaintiffs and I made many trips back and forth to Washington, D.C., at our own expense.   Since we had all been discriminated against economically, and none of us had much by way of financial reserves, the hardship for us was immense. Additionally, every time we traveled, we were, of course, not farming. A double whammy—no income, exorbitant financial outlay. For a period, two or three times a month, we would make the journey to our nation's capital to meet with our attorneys and with Congresspersons, to make appearances in court, to attend protest marches that were being held in the capital, and to attend to other lawsuit related business. The cost of each trip exceeded $600. With inflation, today, that would be around $1000. Airline tickets, hotel rooms, meals, train and/or taxi services—it all added up. Usually, we were informed that we needed to be in Washington, D.C. for a meeting with little notice so air travel was the only option for us. Flying directly into one of the D.C. airports was cost prohibitive. Therefore, we would fly into BWI in Baltimore and take a train from there. Otherwise, whenever there was enough time, we would drive together to defray some of the costs. Eddie Ross would start out in Mississippi, pick up Lloyd Shaffer, and then swing through Alabama to pick me up. Next, we would stop in Georgia for Lucious Abrams and then in North Carolina for Tim Pigford.[126] We would pack what food we could and share a hotel room. Our common purpose bonded us together, akin to troops in battle. Nevertheless, the stress of this battle affected us all. My friend Lloyd said that his hair started falling out during the lawsuit. In fact, he did not live long after settling with the United States government. We all thought the stress shortened his life.

Amidst growing allegations of widespread racial discrimination by the USDA, Secretary of Agriculture Daniel Glickman ordered a USDA Civil Rights Action Team to investigate the claims. The resulting report showed that "minority farmers have lost significant amounts of land and potential farm income as a result of discrimination."[127] Between the years of 1983 and 1996, USDA Office of Civil Rights discrimination claims were not being processed due to budget cuts imposed by the Reagan administration.[128]   The office was reopened in 1996 under President Bill Clinton.[129]   Secretary Glickman himself acknowledged, "an awful lot of drawers were filled with complaints that nobody looked at" over the previous 15 to 20 years.[130] Pearlie Reed, who acted as Assistant Secretary of Agriculture in 1997-1998, led the Civil Rights Action Team which made ninety-two recommendations for improvements.[131] Secretary Glickman also shared his concerns in a letter to Inspector General Roger C. Viadero, in response to his report on the civil rights issues within the USDA. Glickman admitted, "I am deeply concern [sic] about allegations that USDA is not delivering its programs in ways that live up to the spirit and letter of the relevant civil rights laws, regulations, and policies of the United States."[132] He also stated that Viadero's report "does confirm that the program discrimination complaint process at the Farm Service Agency lacks integrity, direction, and accountability."[133] Thus, the USDA itself had documented the widespread racial discrimination in their agricultural programs.

During one of our trips in the summer of 1998, Tim, Lloyd and I met with President Bill Clinton along with our Congressional representatives and representatives from the USDA to discuss the plight of Black farmers in the South, our experiences, and the lawsuit. I had an opportunity to address the President directly at which time I shared how we were being treated as Black farmers in America. I informed President Clinton how unfair the system had been to us and to many other African Americans. Being a Black sheriff from Alabama lent a greater impact to my testimony, I believe, and perhaps this is why I felt an extra weight of responsibility to press on on behalf of other African American farmers. President Clinton offered his support to us in our efforts to obtain justice. We were elated! Finally, we were making progress. However, later, once Congress became more involved, the Senators seemed to adopt a different point of view toward African Americans and our farming crisis. Apparently, there was only so much the executive branch could do.

For our visit with President Clinton, I had taken a few jars of my Hall's Homemade Syrup as a gift. I thought our president, a fellow Southerner, would appreciate a taste of a product from our home region. President Clinton's assistant, Bob Nash, sent me a thank you note shortly thereafter, stating how much he and the President had enjoyed the syrup. I also felt honored to pose for a photograph with both President Clinton and Vice President Al Gore. Meeting with the President and with congresspersons and attending marches were all quite exciting, but truthfully, I would have rather been home on my farm. Like President George Washington who dreamed of returning to Mount Vernon the entire time he served as President but felt his duty to his country was greater, I felt as though I had a duty to see that the lawsuit was successful on behalf of the hundreds, even thousands, of Black farmers whose livelihoods had been damaged by the FmHA, no matter how much I preferred my Alabama farm.

In addition to our many trips to Washington, D.C., once we had filed our class action suit, Tim Pigford, Lloyd Shaffer, and I traveled throughout the South to inform other farmers that they might have recourse if they had been discriminated against by the USDA. We met with Black farmers in Alabama, Mississippi, Georgia, North Carolina, and South Carolina. In each state, we met with the Federation of Southern Cooperatives. We met at land grant colleges and universities and visited African American churches. We wanted to inform other Black farmers that they were not alone in their experiences. With others joining our lawsuit, they would add weight to our claims as well. For their part, the attorneys for our case ran ads in Jet magazine, on radio, and on television. All these trips around the South were at our own expense. Representatives from other states also came to some of our meetings and took the information regarding the lawsuit back to their communities. In addition, Tuskegee University informed members of the Black farming community that there was recourse if they had been discriminated against. All told, we were on the road for about a full year. Throughout that time, we attempted to get our case before the judge with a jury, but we never achieved that.

Of course, road trips with my fellow plaintiffs and friends allowed us ample time to discuss the progress of our case. On one of our many road trips as the lawsuit continued, we debated among ourselves as to how this thing was unfolding. We concurred it was not unfolding in our favor. We were driving to Mississippi for another meeting with potential victims of racial discrimination at the hands of local representatives of the FmHA. By this point, I had begun to feel that attorneys like Pires had greater interest in making a name for themselves and obtaining a large financial payout for themselves than they did in fighting for us. Tim, on the other hand, believed strongly that Pires and others had our best interests at heart, that they were fair, and that they would win for us. Usually, we harmonized well together, but this one discussion became heated—so much so that we needed to pull over, walk off our tension, and compose ourselves before we agreed to disagree and returned to our travels. Lloyd told me confidentially that he tended to agree with me and my position, but he refused to openly disagree with Tim. I cannot say whether Lloyd meant it or if he was merely peacekeeping. I can't say as I blame him either way. Unity amongst us was crucial. We were allies fighting a common battle, and we could not allow dissension to deter us from our mission.

Chapter 16

Settlement

After a lengthy preparation for the case to go to trial or to reach a settlement from August 1997 when we first filed to the Spring of 1999, the United States government and our attorney Pires crafted a consent decree agreement. We, the lead plaintiffs, disagreed with what they produced for us. However, as 1997 melded into 1998 and then the case wore on into 1999, Tim Pigford, Lloyd Shaffer, and I believed with increasing certainty that the lawsuit would crash down upon us. We feared we might not even be able to recoup the money we had outlaid for all our travels. I believe that the lawsuit expanded in ways Pires, Fraas, and the other attorneys involved had not foreseen. It snowballed and seemed to me too big for them to handle. The more Black farmers that joined the lawsuit, the more expensive the case became to prosecute. We felt less certain that our attorneys were interested in representing us and sensed they were more interested in their own financial benefit and reducing their workload. Sometimes it even felt as though our attorneys were on the government's side! Of course, I cannot speak to what transpired in the minds of our legal counsel. Pires had spoken to Congress about how angry he was on our behalf. I just know how I felt at the time and how frustrated I had become with the entire legal process. Both Tim and Lloyd also came to the same conclusion, that Pires and other attorneys were working primarily for themselves as a job and not primarily for us, the clients. We thought it seemed as though if they could get us to settle, then they would be assured a profit. This was their livelihood, after all. For our parts, possible bankruptcy weighed us down. We feared bankruptcy due to the financial burden upon us with all the travel week after week and the time away from farming. We had no way of knowing if we would win or win enough to even cover our expenses. Pires met with Tim, Lloyd, and me. Caught between a rock and a hard place, and strapped for funds, we each decided to take our attorney's advice to opt out of the lawsuit and settle.

Although our attorneys had often treated us as a collective group throughout this lawsuit process, when it came time to hammer out a settlement, they met with each of us individually. I remember sitting at the negotiating table with my attorneys while across from us sat the government's attorneys. Only one Black man—the government's handpicked arbitrator—sat on the government's side. When one of the government attorneys asked me, "What can I do for you?" I thought for a minute. Emotions welled up unbidden. I tried to compose myself but was unable to. I broke down and began to cry. Now, I have demonstrated for civil rights in a dangerous town in Alabama. I have fought in Vietnam. I have served as military police, a police officer, and a sheriff. Crying does not come naturally to me. And yet, here, now... it was all too much. Memories of being pulled over by the police on the way back from Selma, of the pennies in the courthouse, and of my civil rights disputes with the City of Eutaw and the Alabama National Guard, and the many instances of racial discrimination against me by the USDA and the battles I had fought with them flooded through my body and mind.

Although the United States government, this megalithic giant of a defendant, had wronged me and many, many other African American farmers, and although they admitted as much, I knew that they still did not want to make proper restitution toward us. They wanted it to go away. The magnitude of the crisis was so great and even a partial restitution would cost the government a tremendous sum of money which they would not relish paying out, even though African Americans continued to have so many economic opportunities robbed from them. As I sat there, I realized that to continue fighting against this gigantic government would be like fighting with one hand tied behind my back. I am a fighter in my spirit, but this? How could I continue to take on the USDA? It seemed impossible. The USDA and the judicial system seemed a white structured monstrosity of racial partiality and discrimination. Even now, only one Black face sat across the table from me. Here I was spending money I did not have and could not afford to part with, to fight for what I believed a righteous cause. But the defendant? The government had access to unlimited resources—lawyers, researchers, paralegals—and seemingly no limit to the amount of money they could throw at the case—my own and other farmers' tax dollars being used to fight against us. My own tax dollars were helping to pay the salaries of all the people sitting across from me! I and other Black citizens were giving them the tools and the funds to fight us, even as we sought justice from them.

How? How could I win? Tim, Lloyd, and I had advised our attorney that we did not approve of the proposed settlement. However, it appeared to us that our attorneys had in a sense joined forces with the government. Our lawyers favored a speedy settlement which would allow them to win the largest lawsuit against the USDA and one of the largest lawsuits in history against the United States with the minimum of time and effort involved on their parts, in comparison to what it would take to seek justice in a trial. Again, I cannot know what they thought and felt. Perhaps they really had worked the best deal they could, knowing the legal system as they did. But after all we had been through, it seemed insufficient. Of course, in a dispute, one must compromise, and each side surrenders something it wants. Indeed, I did feel as though this was a surrender. Nevertheless, I was traversing uncharted territory and sensed there were minefields and other traps ahead, though I knew not where. A cease-fire. A surrender. Yes. I decided it would be in my best interest to salvage what I could from this nightmarish situation. Reluctantly, I accepted an agreement. My hope was that I had reached an end to one of the most profoundly emotionally and physically exhausting periods of my life. I signed on April 14, 1999, and that same day federal District Court Judge Friedman approved the consent decree.

Tim Pigford settled as well, and so did Lloyd Shaffer. Thus, the three original plaintiffs in the largest civil suit against the U.S. government dropped out, and the original class-action lawsuit bearing Tim Pigford's name ended. The other lead plaintiffs would need to settle independently. Eventually, thousands had come forward to file their claims against "the Last Plantation"—as we in the Black farming community frequently called the USDA—with Poorman-Douglas Corporation, which acted as facilitator.[134] The scheduled deadline was October 12, 1999. In total, as of 2012, 22,721 claimants were considered eligible for participation in the claims process. In all, 22,551 claims were decided under the Track A provision. A full 31% of claims—6,906—were denied. They could not pass the bar set for showing they had likely been discriminated against.[135] Only 169 claimants pursued Track B, and only 104 of them demonstrated to the government's satisfaction that there was a preponderance of evidence indicating they had been discriminated against.[136] These were high hurdles for some claimants to leap because they lacked access to USDA records and therefore had difficulty showing that they had been treated substantially differently than similarly situated white farmers. A full 38% of these Track B claims failed.[137] The lawsuit provided over a billion dollars in cash payments to farmers who were ultimately approved from Tracks A and B.[138] The payments were meant to cover debt relief and cash relief, with additional funds to cover the tax payments they would owe after settlement.[139]

Later, many would claim that they had not known about the class action lawsuit until after the deadline was passed. I never could quite wrap my mind around the idea that so many did not know about the lawsuit in time to file. Tim, Lloyd, and I had worked so hard to get the word out. We had alerted Southern Co-ops, land grant universities and colleges, and had met at some local churches. Perhaps if we had visited more local churches? Also, the attorneys had advertised. Nevertheless, many were unable to make claims in time. Because of those delayed claims, in 2008, Congress included a provision in the farm bill extending the deadline for application to the Pigford lawsuit so those who had filed after the cutoff date could still have their claims adjudicated. Congress allocated up to $1.25 billion to meet those farmers' claims in the class action lawsuit known as Pigford II. A Congressional Research Service report estimated that around 50% or so of the claimants would qualify after their cases were examined.[140] By August 2013, more than another billion dollars, as previously allocated, had been paid to the 17,000 additional claimants who had filed under Pigford II.[141] Pigford II was finalized on January 10, 2018 when U.S. District Court Judge Paul Friedman decreed that the remaining funds approved by Congress for the

Pigford II settlements would be granted to nonprofit farming organizations.[142] I had long been out of the battle by then.

Regarding the number of African Americans who filed claims in Pigford I and Pigford II, some have insisted that there was widespread fraud. They have used the agricultural census data to claim that more African Americans filed than there were African American farmers in the nation. However, those crying fraud misunderstand the agricultural census data. The censuses counted only those who were principal operators of farms and did not include those who farmed cooperatively. It is conceivable that partnerships of several African American farmers worked a particular property but only the principal operator would be counted for census purposes. All may have attempted to obtain loans from the USDA at some point over the period covered by the Pigford class action suit.[143] Also, African Americans could sublease land owned by a principal operator, Black or white, but only the principal operator/ owner would have been counted in the agricultural census. Others who were entitled to file included those who had attempted to farm but had been denied loans on account of their race and therefore never had the opportunity and also those who petitioned on behalf of the estate of a deceased relative who had farmed or attempted to farm but had encountered the USDA's racial discrimination.[144] Thus, the numbers of Black farmers eligible to file claims exceeded the numbers of Black farmers counted in the censuses throughout the 1980s and 1990s. Could there have been fraud? Sure. A case like this may have attracted a few opportunists. However, close to a third of claimants were denied settlements in Pigford I and many more were denied settlements in Pigford II. It is more likely, in my opinion, that some of those denied had legitimate claims but lacked the ability to demonstrate their validity. That said, I personally felt wounded when I learned that those who had turned their backs on me after I had filed a racial discrimination complaint against the Farm Service Agency (former FmHA) in 1995, later jumped on board the Black farmers' lawsuit. On a positive note, most of those who had believed the slander against me did eventually come back around as the truth of my claims was proven again and again.

My own settlement provided $175,000 cash relief for myself and $61,250 to cover the taxes for which I would be liable ($236,250 total cash payout).[145] It also provided me with debt forgiveness for my outstanding loan with the Farm Service Agency (FSA) and promised coverage of my legal fees.[146] There were additional provisions that ensured that for five years from settlement I would have priority financial and technical assistance from the USDA for programs for which I qualified, flexibility in deciding with which FSA officials I would work, and priority consideration for acquisition of additional land, should I choose to lease or purchase some.[147] Thankfully, the settlement would cover my financial outlay for all the travel I had engaged in with the frequent meetings in Washington, D.C. and the trips throughout the South to alert others to their right to file a claim if they had also experienced any discrimination. Additional expenses I had incurred included massive photocopying and mailings of documents for the lawsuit. However, I had missed much time away from my farm and the income I should have been generating there. And, honestly, it did not begin to cover the emotional, mental, and physical wear and tear I had endured.

Chapter 17

New Loan Officer, New Battles

While I was engaged in the Black farmers' lawsuit, I was elected as the first President of the Tuskegee University Cooperative Extension Program Advisory Council in February 1998.[148] In August of the same year, Heifer Project International presented me with the Golden Achievement Award for services rendered to the community.[149] Later in 1999, before the federal government and I reached settlement in the lawsuit, Tuskegee University Cooperative Extension Program awarded me with the T. M. Campbell Leadership Award for "demonstrating persistent efforts to reach out and extend educational and economic development opportunities for others to help themselves."[150] The validation of my hard work, farming expertise, and community support during the trying lawsuit period was most welcome.

After reaching the settlement agreement, I was anxious to return my full-time focus to farming. With the executed settlement agreement showing I had been cleared of debt to the USDA FSA and granting me priority financial and technical assistance, I was entitled to receive my property deeds. During the week of April 18, 1999, I visited the local Greene/Sumter USDA FSA office and requested the FSA release my property mortgage and deliver my deeds to me.[151] For months, I had been planning on installing an irrigation system for my vegetable farms to mitigate the damage to my farming operations from the frequent drought conditions in the southeast United States. I needed the deeds so I could use them as collateral for a loan for the irrigation system.[152] After all I had been through, I preferred to obtain a loan from a private bank rather than enter into another farm loan with the Greene/Sumter FSA office. However, the FSA continued to hold the deed for property purchased under the FmHA for what they referred to as administrative reasons, even after the loan was considered paid in full via the USDA's recent settlement agreement with me.

I continued to request my deeds from FSA which they should have released in accordance with my Pigford v. Glickman settlement. Time was of the essence for my farming operation, and the business opportunity was slipping away. I escalated my request for release of my deeds to the state FSA and national USDA offices.[153] The national officials in Washington, D.C. advised me to return to the Greene/Sumter County FSA office and request a loan if I needed funds immediately.[154] Reluctantly, before April 1999 ended, I requested a loan from the local FSA for my irrigation system. I advised the loan officer that I was entitled to priority technical and financial assistance per the settlement agreement signed earlier that month. She told me, regardless of the settlement, I would not receive any special privilege from their office. I became increasingly frustrated that the same people who had discriminated against me all along had retained their jobs. They exuded an attitude of retribution towards me, and I felt certain that they were trying to get even with me for filing suit. I had, after all, shed light upon their discriminatory practices and demonstrated the widespread racial prejudice and discrimination throughout the office up the entire supervisory chain. Their every action led me to believe that they planned to show me I still had not won.

Although I requested the loan in April 1999, they did not approve the loan and release the funds until August 23, 1999.[155] The Greene/Sumter County FSA office had not retired their old tricks. Not only was it far too late for me to install and utilize the irrigation for the 1999 planting season, but they had also reduced the loan amount by 15%. The final approved loan amount was $34,000, and loan payments amounted to $6,145, due August 1st of each year until I fulfilled the loan obligation.[156] The funds proved insufficient to acquire the equipment needed to properly install the irrigation system I had envisioned.[157] I was forced to compromise and install an inferior system which would not fully meet the farm's needs.[158] Furthermore, without the irrigation system in place for the 1999 season, Hall Farm once again experience crop disaster. The U.S. government had again declared our area a natural disaster due to drought, and I had had no irrigation system in place to mitigate the drought's effects on my crops.[159]

One of the new local loan officers, a young black woman with whom I would primarily work, visited my farm for a chattel check. She appeared hostile towards me. I pressed her as to why she appeared to be at odds with me. She replied, "I am just following orders." Ironically, she was hired to increase racial diversity in the FSA after the myriad of discrimination complaints by Black farmers. Now, to keep her job, she seemed intent on perpetuating the discrimination and hostility toward me which originally had led to the Pigford v. Glickman lawsuit. Although I had clearly demonstrated the discrimination I had faced, her supervisor apparently poisoned her opinion of me.

I cannot begin to express the level of emotional distress this caused me. I was severely disappointed in her. I had fought for civil rights for Black Americans my whole life so that other Black Americans could obtain decent jobs and freely practice their rights. She had benefited from the efforts of civil rights fighters like me but seemed utterly oblivious to the sacrifices we made for her generation. She and other members of the local FSA office spoke rudely to me in every subsequent interaction. In this manner, the USDA continued to breach the terms of our settlement agreement. One condition had been that I would not be required to work with the same local USDA servicing personnel against whom I had been forced to file complaints. Even though I was now interacting with this new loan officer, since she was acting as an extension of those with whom I had had prior conflict, in effect, nothing had changed.

Unfortunately, drought conditions continued to prevail in Alabama in the summers of 2000 and 2001. After natural disaster had been declared for 1999, the USDA FSA sent notifications to farmers dated November 30, 1999, of a disaster set-aside program. I applied and was thankfully approved without conflict on July 27, 2000.[160]

Despite the ongoing drought conditions during the second half of the summer of 2000, I paid my loan installment. Because 2000 had been declared a drought year as well, FSA allowed farmers to apply for emergency loans due to crop losses in 2000. I applied for an emergency loan on February 23, 2001, at my local FSA office in advance of the application deadline. The emergency loan was specifically for farmers who had suffered financial distress due to the 2000 drought disaster. The loan officer refused my request for the loan for which I qualified.[161] Then "on March 14, 2001, I signed up for the 2000 crop disaster program."[162] While the USDA did pay me for all crops reported as losses, as before, one of my high- volume crop yields—for sorghum, one of my major crops—was reduced significantly.[163] This was another blow. First the emergency loan denial and now this? Two years since the settlement and little had changed. Although I successfully challenged the unreasonable crop yield reduction and the USDA reversed its initial decision, the FSA delayed the payment for over two years, which significantly impacted my farm's finances.[164]

As I surveyed my crops in 2001, I realized my crops would once again fail due to drought. According to USDA FSA regulations (7 CFR 1951.906), a borrower is delinquent after failure to make a full or partial payment within 30 days after the due date.[165] July passed, then August arrived, and the drought continued. Within a week and a half of the first day of August, I contacted my loan officer at the Greene/Sumter County FSA office.[166] Although she consistently proved difficult to work with, I had no choice. I explained that due to the drought conditions, I would not be able to make my loan payment that month and needed to reschedule.[167] Technically, I had become a financially distressed borrower and as such, I exercised my right to Primary Loan Servicing, meaning we would need to restructure my loan.[168] I knew that according to USDA FSA rules, it was crucial to begin the application process within 30 days of the expected default. If I did not apply promptly, I would become a delinquent borrower, and the rules for loan restructuring would then become much more stringent.

On August 27, 2001, I submitted my application for Primary Loan Servicing within the allotted time frame to the Greene/Sumter County Alabama FSA office. They accepted it.[169] In a letter dated the following day, the loan officer requested additional information for my loan application relating to my real estate holdings, any property leases or rent obligations and my current debt and credit information. I quickly assembled the requested information and sent it in to the FSA office within a couple days to expedite the Primary Loan Servicing process.[170]

On September 6, 2001, the loan officer visited Hall's Farm and requested tax returns and my production data. I explained to her that the FSA already had my latest tax returns for 1999 on file. I had filed for an extension for Hall's Farm's 2000 taxes. While she waited, I submitted a copy of my 2000 tax extension form to her. I promised her my production data shortly.[171] While at my farm, the loan officer indicated that I would be required to pledge property to proceed with the restructuring process. While she should have known the FSA's rules, I explained to her that as a financially distressed current borrower having made application within the grace period, I was not required to produce additional assets as collateral. That applied only in situations of delinquency.[172] Within a couple days of our meeting, I delivered production data to the FSA office. The FSA loan officer now had my completed application, and we could work together on a feasible restructuring plan.

The loan officer subverted the process. In a letter dated September 26, 2001, she stated that she had suspended processing on my 1951-S application for primary loan servicing for financially distressed borrowers.[173] And...as per my request!? No way! Immediately I called her office to clarify that at no time had I requested suspension of my application. Again, she attempted to convince me that I would need to pledge property. Again, I explained that requirement pertained only to delinquent borrowers. I had not been a delinquent borrower at the time of my application on August 27, nor when she requested additional information on August 28. Regulations allowed an applicant 60 days to provide additional documents as needed to the FSA office as attachments to the application. I had complied with all requests.[174] She agreed to reinstate the application and did so on October 18, 2001, granting the 60 days to complete the application.[175] After our conversation, however, she failed to make any substantial effort to process my application.

Eventually, I complained to the Secretary of Agriculture, letting the USDA personnel in the Washington, D.C. offices know that the local FSA office refused to comply with the settlement agreement that the U.S. government had made with me. On October 22, 2001, in a complaint letter (OCR Case #1222569), I explained that the loan officer and local FSA office had failed to service my farm loan restructure as a financially distressed current borrower. They advised me to return to the local FSA office for whatever services I needed.[176] The local loan officer became increasingly defiant. At one point during our contentious relationship, she had flat out told me that I would not get any preference from their office in meeting my legitimate farming needs despite that being a requirement of the USDA FSA settlement.

On November 16, 2001, the Farm Service Agency sent me Instruction 1951-S, "Notice of the Availability of Loan Servicing and Debt Settlement Programs for Delinquent Farm Borrowers."[177] Once again, I explained to the loan officer that I qualified for Primary Loan Servicing as a financially distressed current borrower because I had applied within the appropriate time frame. Left with little recourse, I corresponded with my attorney's office, explaining the current circumstances I faced. Pires's office had crafted the Pigford v. Glickman lawsuit and my settlement agreement, and I thought he would represent me in my efforts to have the settlement honored. I received no response. Additional attempts to contact Pires's office were met with a cold shoulder. Although he had crafted and signed the agreement, now his approach toward my legal needs seemed hands off. I wrote and advised him of his fiduciary responsibility towards me. Surely, he could assist me or direct Fraas to? But he did not intervene on my behalf.

Despite the ongoing conflict, in December 2001, the farming community chose me to be the first elected African American to serve on the United States Department of Agriculture, Farm Service Agency of Greene/Sumter County Committee in Eutaw, Alabama. As I had seen, members of the local FSA committees were integral to the administration of USDA policies and programs. Having suffered because of poor leadership in our local FmHA (FSA) Committee, I sought to bring fairness to the organization for those farmers who wished to participate in USDA programs. Rather than seeking retaliation against those who had tried to harm me, and still seemed eager to do so, I lived out my faith. The teachings of Jesus Christ and the holy scriptures compel me to treat both friends and enemies with fairness. Because I love Jesus and am committed to living my life in accordance with His words, I needed to act in love even toward those who had hurt me.[178] Integrity matters. I could not do to others as they had done to me but desired to model the Golden Rule and treat others as I myself would like to be treated.[179] Being elected in 2001 provided me with a sense of vindication, that my struggle was not in vain. I was proud to have blazed a trail and become the first African American elected outright to this role in our community. Other members of the committee seemed to respect me. I believe they understood that I had been treated unfairly. In contrast to the FSA employees, the elected committee members seemed to bear me no ill will or resentment now that the two troublesome members had been removed. As a committee member, my duties, as stated in Greene County's "The Democrat," would include:

- Making policy decisions on county program administration.

- Ensuring farmer and public understanding of FSA programs.

- Developing and carrying out active outreach programs.

- Promoting good working relations with other agricultural agencies.

- Making recommendations to the state FSA Committee on needed changes in programs and their administration.

- Conducting hearings and reviews as needed or requested by the state FSA Committee.

- Providing a workplace environment free from discrimination.

- Avoiding the appearance of a conflict of interest.[180]

Chapter 18

Different Loan Officer, Same Battles

Eventually, I requested that my loan officer be replaced with a new loan officer, and the FSA assigned James E. Currington to my case.[181] Unfortunately, Currington appeared intent on covering up for the former loan officer's failures to properly process my application, and he continued the local FSA's ill treatment toward me.[182] Between August 2001 and March 2002, I submitted seven Farm and Home Plans to the Greene/Sumter FSA office. Each time, the loan officer determined that the plan was not feasible. They accepted none of them.[183] We attempted mediation on May 29, 2002, but once again, they refused to approve my restructuring request, citing a lack of a feasible plan of operation.[184] On June 10, 2002, after an eighth and final attempt to provide them with a Farm and Home Plan, FSA informed me that their Debt and Loan Restructuring System analysis indicated Hall's Farm's plan of operation was not feasible.[185]

Currington, the Acting Farm Loan Manager Richard Nazary, and I convened for a reconsideration meeting on August 8, 2002.[186] Again, we talked through my Farm and Home Plan. I asked about the Softwood Timber Program I had heard about which would enhance my farm's profitability. They stated that I was not entitled to the Softwood Timber Program option.[187] We made no headway, and after a year of battle, I left the meeting crestfallen. A few days later, I received a letter from Currington with their final decision. It reaffirmed their position that my Farm and Home Plan did not demonstrate that Hall's Farm would be profitable enough to cover farm operation expenses, family living expenses and the scheduled debt repayments.[188] Currington directed me to appeal to the National Appeals Division (NAD) if I still believed their decision incorrect.[189]

Although news of their final decision devastated me, I could not believe there were no other options. I contacted the National FSA Loan Servicing Office in Washington, D.C. about the Softwood Timber Program's laws and regulations. Upon learning more, I realized that this absolutely should have been considered an option, yet the Greene/Sumter FSA office had just brushed my inquiry aside. Yes, I would appeal their decision to the NAD. On August 15, 2002, I sent a letter to the National Appeals Division's Southern Regional Office in Tennessee, appealing the loan officer's decision. I had been through this process before, so I carefully laid out my analysis regarding the error of their decision. They had not processed my Primary Loan Servicing application in a timely manner, causing my loan to become delinquent through no fault of my own. I indicated that I had reason to believe their decision against me was based on their own bias, a desire to cover up their initial mistakes, and a desire for retribution against me. And then I waited.

In October 2002, a representative from the USDA's National Appeals Division (NAD) contacted me. My case number was 2002S001180. On October 15, 2002, we had a prehearing conference and agreed to meet in person to conduct an appeal hearing two weeks later, on October 28 in Montgomery, Alabama.[190] Pat Skaggs acted as the hearing officer.[191] I arrived with my timeline and all my documentation. They had made it abundantly clear that at this point, it was I who bore "the burden of proving by a preponderance of the evidence" that the Greene/Sumter FSA office's adverse decision in my case was erroneous.[192]   Despite having no attorney representation, I believed I had presented a compelling case against the Greene/Sumter FSA office. When the facts are on your side, and those in power are unbiased, doing so is far less complicated.

On November 7, 2002, Skaggs rendered the NAD's appeal determination on my case. In the four-page document, they enumerated the facts of my case, the applicable laws and regulations, and their determination. The document delineated clearly that I had properly submitted my application as a financially distressed current borrower, not as a delinquent borrower, and that the local office had inexplicably suspended my application and reinstated it as a delinquent borrower, against the agency's proper procedures.   In their estimation, the Greene/Sumter FSA office **did** err in its decision![193]   I had won! They stated, of course, that either party could request a review of their determination by a director, but why would I do that? I had presented the facts, and I had finally been heard and vindicated.

Unfortunately, the local FSA office was unwilling to concede their error. They appealed for a director review. James R. Little, an administrator for the USDA FSA, officially requested a director's review on December 2, 2002.[194]   His statement was riddled with false or misleading statements, which I imagine was based on disinformation from the local office.   Among other claims, he stated that my original loan application was incomplete and that I had not provided requested documents.[195]   Later, on January 17, 2003, Little addressed a letter to Roger Klurfeld,

Director of the National Appeals Division, stating "new information has come to light that has caused FSA to determine that Appellant (meaning me) should be given notice of his opportunity to be considered for the Softwood Timber Program. FSA will give Appellant notice of this opportunity and resume its consideration of Appellant's eligibility for Primary Loan Servicing with that step" which suggested that this would solve the problem about which we had been in conflict for almost a year and a half. He continued, "Instead of reversing the hearing officer's decision as previously requested, we instead request that you vacate the hearing officer's decision so that FSA may proceed to give Appellant the necessary additional notice and make a new determination on Appellant's eligibility for Primary Loan Servicing."[196]

In the end, justice once again did not prevail. Director Klurfeld vacated the NAD Hearing Officer's determination and in the Director's Review Determination wrote, "On December 2, 2002, the FSA Acting Administrator submitted a written request for review of the Hearing Officer's determination. In that submission, the Acting Administrator requested that the Hearing Officer's determination be reversed. However, on January 17, 2003, the FSA Administrator notified NAD that because of new information, FSA now requests that the Hearing Officer's determination be vacated so that FSA may make a new determination on appellant's eligibility for Primary Loan Servicing. This position appears to resolve the issue on appeal."[197] Despite my having asked specifically about the Softwood Timber Program and the FSA office informing me I did not qualify, they had now presented this as new information that had just come to light. They had had no intention of assisting me with this program until after they had been ruled against. Then they lied and acted as though this was a new option and that they had every intention of working with me in good faith. This further convinced me that the entire year and a half long harassment and their refusal to work with me was based on a desire for retribution for all the times I had stood against inherent and systemic racism, including my involvement in the Pigford v. Glickman case, as if I needed any further proof. They had won after all. I was forced to continue trying to work with the same office that had told me I would receive no help from them, despite the Pigford v. Glickman settlement which entitled me to priority assistance.

Chapter 19

A Life-Altering Night

One evening in 2002, amid the ongoing strife with the local FSA office, I had left the Hall's Homemade Syrup building and had begun walking home just as I had countless other nights. As I approached the house, an overwhelming exhaustion overtook me. "Good heavens," I thought to myself. "Why am I so tired?" I had ceased my daily habit of running for a while by that point. Clearly, I had become out of shape. Being used to disciplining myself, I decided I should begin whipping myself into shape immediately. I ran a lap around my house. I was even more tired. "Try another lap," I said to myself. When I finished the second lap, I entered my home. Under the weight of extreme exhaustion, I dragged myself to my reclining chair to rest. However, relief did not come, and my chest began to hurt. Indigestion, I figured. I felt terribly ill. However, thinking there was nothing wrong that would not right itself by morning, I said nothing to my wife Janetta. I just reclined in the chair all night.

The next morning, I felt no better. The chest pain had persisted throughout the night. At that point, I visited my family physician, and complained about the severe chest pain. I explained that I thought I had indigestion. My doctor knew me well and after examining me agreed that there was probably nothing seriously wrong with me. Although I had recently discontinued my usual exercise routine, I remained in good physical shape. I was still slim and ate well. He gave me medication for heartburn to settle the acid.

I returned home and took the acid relieving medication as directed. However, the medicine did not give me any relief. The next morning, I returned to my doctor's office and complained that the pain had not abated and had instead become excruciating. My doctor appeared startled. He informed me that it might be my heart. He called a cardiologist with whom he worked and secured me an appointment for the following day with the specialist.

The cardiologist was excellent. He said he could tell me what was wrong even before examining me, although he proceeded to examine me anyway. He said that the pain I was suffering was called angina. He suspected I had heart disease, specifically atherosclerosis, meaning my arteries were clogged or there were blockages. Therefore, the blood was not circulating properly. Fortunately, they had a procedure that could help me. He referred me for bloodwork and scheduled cardiac catheterization for me which would confirm his initial diagnosis. He told me that if they found the blockages he was describing, they could insert stents. Stents, he explained, would help keep my arteries open and improve blood flow.

I underwent the procedure as scheduled. While it is always scary to undergo procedures under anesthesia, I knew I was in good hands—the Lord's and the doctor's. Unfortunately, they found my arteries were too small to insert stents. Therefore, the cardiologist discussed other options with me. He prescribed me blood thinning and cholesterol lowering medications and instructed me to eat more fruits and vegetables and to avoid fast foods. Of course, I had long followed the healthy eating part of this equation. He advised me to return after a few weeks so he could reexamine me and see how the medical interventions were working. If I had not improved, he would refer me to a high-tech medical center which would be able to insert stents despite my small arteries.

I followed all the cardiologist's recommendations. My brother also suggested I see Dr. Howard, a physician he knew, who performed chelation treatments. Chelation therapy is used to bind with heavy metals such as mercury or lead in a person's bloodstream, allowing them to excrete the heavy metal toxins through the urinary system. Some believed that chelation therapy could also help reduce the risks and severity of heart disease. In chelation therapy, I learned, they insert an IV and inject a chelating agent to bind with the heavy metals to flush them out. In the case of atherosclerosis, proponents believed, the chelating agent would bind with calcium in the arteries and flush out both the calcium and other debris. I figured this procedure was worth a try too, so I underwent twenty-five chelation therapy treatments in Demopolis, Alabama. With the chelation treatments, I felt so much better. I believe they helped removed some of the plaque from my arteries.

After the allotted time had expired in which to try the interventions the cardiologist had recommended, I returned to his office. He saw significant improvement and was pleased with my progress. He allowed me to continue with the medication and diet and whatever I was doing. I had not told him about the chelation therapy, but I believe it had been an important part of my improved condition. I also continued to take the medications he had prescribed. Later, I was diagnosed with several other diseases, all of which are associated with Agent Orange exposure. Since heart disease had also been linked to Agent Orange exposure during the Vietnam War, my cardiac issues made more sense to me. I had always stayed physically active and eaten a heart-healthy diet, so why had I developed heart disease? Agent Orange seemed the likely culprit. When I had first been diagnosed with heart disease, it was not recognized as part of a syndrome of infirmities associated with that chemical. However, over time the professionals saw the correlation and concluded heart disease was another result of exposure. Agent Orange related health concerns forced me to severely limit my normal activities. Over time, I could not perform any significant physical labor without experiencing angina. Loving physical activity as I do, this has sometimes been exceedingly difficult for me to bear. Yet, I bear all things through Christ who strengthens me.

Chapter 20

New Legal Challenges

Throughout the recent conflicts with the FSA, I had contacted Pires and Fraas about the ongoing problems, but they failed to assist me in enforcing the settlement agreement. Based on my understanding, they were still supposed to represent me after the settlement was signed, and at no time had I signed documents releasing the attorneys from representing me. I also sought the assistance of local attorneys to file for breach of contract, but they advised me to contact the attorneys who had originally represented me as they had received payment for representing me in the lawsuit. Duly, I had advised Pires repeatedly of the USDA's breach of contract and asked for either him or Fraas to intervene on my behalf, specifically to rectify their violation of the agreement and the disparity of treatment I had received. But neither Pires nor Fraas intervened to assist me in resolving the ongoing dispute, even though this was still their job, as I understood it. Finally, I filed a complaint with the D.C. Chapter of the American Bar Association against Fraas and Pires on September 16, 2003, about a half year before the settlement was due to expire.[198] With my law enforcement experience, I felt confident in my ability to file. I contended that they had violated the rules of professional conduct. Unfortunately, after communicating with the attorneys' offices, the D.C. American Bar Association Chapter apparently did not agree with my position and allowed the attorneys to release me as a client. They indicated that they need not continue representing me in this ongoing legal matter. They faced no penalties.

Without the help of an attorney, I remained unable to obtain the assistance from my local FSA to which I was entitled. Finally, the five-year settlement period provided for in my Pigford v. Glickman settlement expired. Frustrated that the local FSA had succeeded in ignoring the settlement agreement and with their ongoing rudeness towards me, I once again sought help from local attorneys. No one wanted to become involved. Continuing to seek justice, on May 12, 2004, I filed a complaint pro se for breach of agreement and retaliation against the United States Department of Agriculture in the United States District Court for the Northern District of the State of Alabama Western Division.[199] The case number was CV-04-CO-0971-W. As I prepared my complaint against the USDA, Sam Taylor spoke with me a couple times to give me some pointers. However, the filing was my work. I tried to be as thorough as possible. I requested a jury trial, having determined that that would be the best way for me to have a chance at a truly fair hearing.

In my complaint, I explained my position that the FSA office had retaliated against me for my part in the Pigford v. Glickman lawsuit and had failed to abide by the settlement, beginning immediately with their failure to provide me with priority financial assistance when I sought the loan for the irrigation system in April 1999, providing the loan late (in August) and at a reduced amount.[200] I contended that they continued their retaliation by actively discouraging me from completing an emergency loan application in 2001.[201] Through the disaster relief program, I was entitled to file, along with other farmers in my area of the country, for disaster payments for the 1999 and the 2000 agricultural years. However, just as before, they reduced high volume crop yields and disaster payments, leaving me with no option but to fight up the FSA/USDA system until they reestablished crop yields and made payment.[202] Lastly, in August 2001 when I filed as a financially distressed current borrower, they made improper requests, delayed, and claimed I was then delinquent and no longer eligible for the same programs.[203] In short, I requested the Court find and declare the USDA in breach of our settlement agreement, acknowledge their discriminatory, retaliatory treatment of me and award me whatever relief the Court deemed equitable and just.[204]

The USDA presented the U.S. District Court for the Northern District of the State of Alabama Western Division with a motion to dismiss.[205] They argued that the US District Court lacked subject matter jurisdiction for several of my complaints and that the statute of limitation had been exceeded for several of the problems I had experienced with them.[206] The USDA also argued that since they had, in fact, resolved the disaster relief payment issue, however delayed, there was no other equitable relief available.[207] Finally, the USDA argued that because no employer-employee relationship existed between the USDA and me, based on my citation of Title VII of the Civil Rights Act 42 U.S.C. 1981, my complaint of FSA retaliation against me for filing the Pigford v. Glickman lawsuit against them was invalid.[208]

On November 15, 2004, the United States District Court Northern Alabama District of Alabama Western Division rendered its opinion. It quickly became apparent how difficult it would be to argue in court pro se against a federal agency, even though I had more than the average layperson's knowledge of the legal system. The Court agreed with most of the USDA's arguments. The Court stated that I had failed to demonstrate that it had subject matter jurisdiction in my claim that the USDA had breached our settlement agreement, and they dismissed my complaint.[209] They did, however, indicate that at least some of my complaints could be filed in the Court of Federal Claims, as that would be the court with subject matter jurisdiction.[210] The Court also seemed to concur with the USDA's argument that the statute of limitations had expired for most of my complaints.[211] They agreed with the USDA that because it had reversed itself and paid the disaster relief payments albeit delayed, that point was moot unless I could point to other equitable relief available.[212] Lastly, the Court agreed with the USDA that my citation of Title VII of the Civil Rights Act of 1964 did not cover my claim of retaliation.[213]

Both the USDA and I responded to the Court's November 15, 2004 memorandum of opinion with motion for summary judgment on the outstanding issues before the court.[214] The remaining issues from my original May 2004 complaint were my claims of race discrimination and retaliation. Apparently, my motion for summary judgment was not a proper response to the USDA's motion for summary judgment and the Court determined that I did not respond to the defendant's motion.[215] The USDA claimed that it had properly determined me to be a delinquent borrower. Worse, the Court agreed.[216] This argument made no sense since the USDA itself had determined that the FSA had erred in its decision to treat me as a delinquent borrower and reversed the FSA's decision in November 2002, stating that I had been a financially distressed current borrower and should at no point have been treated as a delinquent borrower.[217] The Court reiterated that I had not, in their opinion, shown race discrimination or that there was any causal link between my participation in the lawsuit and the ongoing difficulties between the FSA office and myself.[218] They saw my settlement in the Pigford Class Action lawsuit in 1999 and their refusal to work appropriately with me in 2001 as too far apart chronologically "to establish the necessary temporal proximity" for retaliation.[219] In summary, on January 31, 2006, the Court granted summary judgment on both the remaining claims from my May 2004 complaint.[220]

In the interim, per the U.S. District Court's suggestion, I filed my complaint (No. 05-517C) in the United States Court of Federal Claims for breach of settlement under the Equal Credit Opportunity Act against the USDA on May 4, 2005. The federal government (USDA) then filed a motion to dismiss this case on July 5, 2005.[221] In their motion to dismiss, they made similar arguments as to the ones in their motion to dismiss in the United States District Court Northern District of Alabama Western Division. Primarily, the government's (USDA's) arguments revolved around jurisdictional issues and expiration of statute of limitations.[222] I filed my response on September 12, 2005, and the Government filed their reply brief on September 19, 2005.[223]

On October 31, 2005, the United States Court of Federal Claims published their Memorandum Opinion and Order. Unlike the United States District Court Northern District of Alabama Western Division, the U.S. Court of Federal Claims held the pleadings of a pro se plaintiff "to a less stringent standard than those of the litigants represented by counsel."[224] Citing Ruderer v United States (1969), the Court said, "Indeed, it has long been the role of this court to examine the record 'to see if [a pro se] plaintiff has a cause of action somewhere displayed.'"[225] This was excellent news for me as a plaintiff after finding that not citing every precedent or applying every legal precept *just so* had caused the U.S. District Court to accept the USDA's motion to dismiss. In contrast, the Court of Federal Claims looked at my complaint holistically, noting that both individually and collectively, my allegations, if true, constituted a breach of the Pigford v. Glickman settlement agreement between the United States government and myself.[226] Of course, this is precisely what I had attempted to argue. In its response, the Court of Federal Claims repeatedly stated it most certainly did have proper jurisdiction to hear my complaint and denied each of the Government's motions to dismiss with the exclusion of for "damages for emotional distress and pain and suffering" because the Court had no authority to award such damages.[227] My case would be permitted to continue. In addition, the Court committed itself to attempt to obtain legal counsel to represent me before them.[228] The legal counsel would be responsible to file a first amended complaint adding a citation of the Tucker Act which would clearly demonstrate the jurisdiction of the United States Court of Federal Claims in this legal matter.[229]

A couple months after the U.S. District Court's opinion, I attended the 114th Annual Farmers Conference at Tuskegee University in February 2006. I spoke publicly at the meeting about my ongoing issues with the USDA's failure to act appropriately after our settlement in the Pigford v. Glickman lawsuit. While there, Rose Sanders, an attorney from Selma, Alabama approached me. She was interested in knowing more about my ongoing dispute with the U.S. government since the settlement. She appeared very sympathetic towards me and my situation. Her law firm, Chestnut, Sanders, Sanders, and Pettaway, had become involved in the Pigford lawsuit as one of the law firms at which farmers could come to file complaints if they believed they had been discriminated against. As we chatted, she indicated that she believed I had been wronged by the government. She also indicated she thought the attorneys had not honored their role in the settlement agreement because they had not continued to represent me when the local FSA office failed to abide by the settlement. She then offered her office's services in my pro se breach of contract claim pro bono if I covered all expenses. This was wonderful news! Of course, I readily agreed, and I handled all the out-of-pocket expenses. I would continue to perform most of the clerical work, and I would pay any costs her office incurred.

Having just received the U.S. District Court Northern District of Alabama's adverse decision, I was ready to appeal. Sanders and I both spoke on the phone and met in person a couple times over the next few months. With her advice, I prepared an appeal of the District Court's decision to the United States Court of Appeals for the Eleventh Circuit. Sanders did appear in court with me at one point to offer me assistance, and as memory serves, it was for this appeal. Then we awaited their response. On November 29, 2006, they decided that I had not established an obvious case of discrimination or retaliation.[230] I believe cases like this demonstrate why so much discrimination and sometimes even retaliation continue. They remain difficult to prove. Even after so many Black farmers like myself had demonstrated the pervasive nature of discrimination in the administration of FSA programs, the courts could not see any evidence of ongoing discrimination or retaliation against me even though the State FSA and the USDA National Appeals Division had had to reverse FSA's decision after the settlement that was supposed to have remedied the unlawful conduct against me.

For her part, Sanders noted several issues with the District Court's rendered opinion and their opinion's ratification by the Eleventh Circuit Court of Appeals which could potentially reverberate through future USDA and FSA decisions. She prepared a petition for rehearing en banc and submitted it to the U.S. Court of Appeals for the Eleventh Circuit on January 16, 2007. First, she argued that not only had the District Court denied my motion for summary judgment on my claim of retaliation by the FSA/USDA against me for my prior litigation, but the District Court initiated a motion to dismiss my case of retaliation without the USDA having made any such motion.[231] Additionally, the District Court dismissed my claim of retaliation based on speculative evidence that had not been presented.[232] This would set a dangerous precedent for the Court if they began arguing the government's case for them and assuming evidence.[233]

Furthermore, Sanders argued in our petition, the U.S. District Court had set a precedent regarding USDA regulations which conflicted with their current regulations and would impact thousands of farmers by allowing inconsistent applications of USDA rules.[234] The USDA clearly establishes a borrower as a current financially distressed borrower if he or she makes application before the loan becomes delinquent, and the borrower then has 60 days to complete the application. The District Court, however, ruled that I had become a delinquent borrower, subject to the more stringent rules for them, on August 31, 2001 because I did not complete the application by then.[235] Even the National Appeals Division of the USDA in Washington, D.C. which fully understood their own agency's rules had declared that I was a current financially distressed borrower and had completed my application within their allotted time frame. The Court's decision would allow for loan officers to break the USDA's own rules as they wished with impunity going forward.[236]

Lastly, Sanders argued that the District Court and the Court of Appeals had ruled in error that there was no evidence of retaliatory behavior.[237] She stated this ruling was in error since there was evidence of the loan officer's unprovoked hostility towards me from the moment I had showed the settlement papers to her.[238] Repeatedly, she had displayed her hostility over the following years, culminating with her demand for collateral for my financially distressed current borrower application, despite there being no such USDA rule, followed by her subsequent inexplicable suspension of my application. Even the USDA's Office of Civil Rights investigator had found the loan officer's behavior troubling.[239] For both Courts to have found no causal link between my prior litigation against the USDA and the adverse actions I suffered thereafter was illogical.[240]

Despite Sanders's valiant efforts to demonstrate that the District Court had misinterpreted the USDA's clearly stated and acknowledged regulations, ignored the USDA's own Office of Civil Rights investigator's acknowledgment that the loan officer's behavior toward me was disturbing, and made several other obvious missteps in their ruling, the Eleventh Circuit Court of Appeals announced their denial of rehearing en banc on March 2, 2007. We had their final word on the matter. They would allow the poor ruling of the lower court to stand. Worse, they would allow dangerous precedents that could affect future cases throughout the United States.[241]

Meanwhile, the concurrent case I had filed (No. 05-517C) had proceeded in the United States Court of Federal Claims. Judge

Susan G. Braden of the U.S. Court of Federal Claims had requested that an attorney named Christopher Danley with Baker Botts LLP, located in Washington, D.C., represent me. He had filed the first amended complaint as directed by the Court. Under his counsel, we worked out a settlement agreement. I signed the agreement on March 26, 2007.[242] My attorney and the U.S. Department of Justice's attorney, Paul Freeborne, signed on March 28, 2007.[243] The agreement, which would supersede my prior Pigford v. Glickman settlement, devastated me. The court ordered that my outstanding loan in the amount of $24,685.09 be forgiven in full.[244] Because the FSA had not released my deeds to me when they were supposed to and had not provided me with the priority technical and loan assistance as had been directed in the 1999 lawsuit, I had been forced to return to the USDA when I needed an additional loan for property and an irrigation system. I would, according to the settlement, be liable for taxation on the loan forgiveness amount. Also, despite the National Appeals Division's concurrence that the local Farm Service Agency's treatment had continued to be inappropriate, the 2007 settlement stated that it did "not constitute an admission of liability or misconduct on the part of the United States, or any agency, officer, or employee thereof."[245]

Lastly, and most damaging to me, this settlement stipulated that I would "be ineligible for any and all future farm ownership, farm operating, and farm emergency loans."[246] I would be precluded from eligibility for future farm loans through the FSA's Farm Loan Programs because the debt cancellation, in the Court's opinion, constituted "debt forgiveness" as defined in the United States Code §§ 1991 (12).[247] In a separate part of the U.S.C. (U.S.C. §§ 2008h(b)), once a farmer is granted debt forgiveness, they are ineligible for future loans.[248] While this provision of the legal code protects the USDA from abuse by large-scale farmers who borrow millions of dollars and occasionally need debt forgiveness, it seems unfair to small-scale farmers who are not defrauding the government out of large sums of money. Of note is that the term "debt forgiveness" does not apply to "any write-down provided as part of a resolution of a discrimination complaint against the Secretary [of Agriculture].[249] Therefore, if the USDA would have admitted that they had discriminated against me, the definition of debt forgiveness would not have been applicable, and I would have continued to have been eligible for future loans from FSA.

Chapter 21

Aftermath

I felt strongly that the U.S. Court of Federal Claims had penalized me for the USDA's wrongdoings. The outcome of the settlement greatly curtailed my ability to farm. Perhaps the court did not fully understand the effect the ineligibility for loans would have upon me as a farmer. However, without operating loans, farming as I had known it was over. No longer could I borrow at the beginning of the season as most farmers do. Most farmers do not have enough capital to purchase seed, fertilizer, and equipment or funds on hand with which to pay workers without these loans. Going forward, the only farming I would be able to perform would be very small-scale, perhaps some vegetable farming. I had to cut back dramatically on the cane and syrup business as well as my beef cattle farming.

When I signed the settlement agreement, I fully understood the ramifications to my farm and to me. I understood what the ineligibility for loans would mean. However, I could not keep fighting. Fighting was too time consuming, and I no longer had the energy to keep fighting the injustices. I had wearied of dealing with the federal government. I knew that they would not admit they had discriminated against me, so pushing for that in the settlement was pointless. I thought, "The hell with this! I've been fighting injustices with the USDA my whole life. I'm done!" From my perspective, the settlement was a bad deal. But I knew nothing would change, and the best deal we could obtain for me would include severing our financial relationship. I was crushed. Shortly thereafter, I received a cordial note from Danley stating it had been an honor to work with me and that with the settlement our attorney-client relationship would end.

To make matters worse, after my claim was settled with the U.S. Court of Federal Claims with Danley as counsel, I received a phone call from Sanders's office requesting that I pay my attorney bill for her work with me on the appeal in the original case I had filed in the U.S. District Court and then in the Court of Appeals. "What attorney bill?" I asked, thoroughly perplexed. "I have never received a bill." I then explained to the office representative that there should be no attorney fees. We had never discussed any fees for attorney work which was supposed to be supplied pro bono, according to my understanding of our original conversation. Over the previous year, I had paid all expenses as we had progressed for documentation, copying, and mailings as well as for any assistance from paralegals along the way. The caller explained why I still owed attorney fees to their offices, but that explanation made no sense to me, and apparently my explanation of pro bono representation made no sense to them either. We had reached an impasse.

After a while, the law office called again. The caller this time was less pleasant. She seemed to insinuate that Black farmers are not trustworthy, and they would never represent a Black farmer again because I would not pay them. I was deeply offended. I had never asked them to represent me. They had voluntarily offered their services pro bono because they had seen that I had been mistreated in the original settlement and its aftermath. I had paid expenses along the way. Regardless, my actions should have no bearing on their relationship with other

Black farmers. That statement sounded blatantly racist. I felt if anyone was untrustworthy, it was they. If Sanders had found that she would need reimbursement, I thought she should have explained that to me. We should have had some agreement along the way stipulating terms and fees for service to avoid misunderstandings like this. However, I had learned my lesson. Trying to reason with them seemed pointless. Sanders had performed work, and if she needed payment for services rendered, I would pay her. I requested that they send me the bill. They sent me a bill which detailed far more than I had expected. While their actions and accusations sorely disappointed me, I paid the bill. Fighting them would be another losing battle, and I wanted no ill will with them over a miscommunication or misunderstanding. This chapter of my life was over. It was time to move on.

I was tired. Tired of fighting. I just wanted to leave all this behind me. I had been in communication with the other lead plaintiffs, and they also faced difficulties with enforcement of their settlements. We concluded that the lawsuit had become a train wreck, having been derailed from its attempts at justice. The years of struggle with the USDA and the FmHA/FSA had drained me, and wearing me down as they had, is a profound, though perverse, achievement. I loved the United States of America and had fought hard for the United States to live up to its ideals and be the country I knew it could be. I had fought in a war for our nation and consequently faced multiple negative health outcomes for my efforts. What had my loyalty to my nation gotten me? I had been wrongfully detained in my youth for bringing coins to pay an illicitly contrived fine and faced years of racial discrimination in farming by the government I had fought to defend. I had been discriminated against in promotions in both my local government and in the Alabama National Guard. As a youth I had believed in the American dream. If I finished school, worked hard, was honest, made good decisions, and invested wisely, I too could be successful. That was the way it was supposed to work. Do the right things and you would be prosperous in the land of the free and the home of the brave.

Now I found myself remembering all the long, lonely nights I had spent over the years contending with discrimination at the hands of the federal government, and I struggled with recurring memories of the terrible combat fighting I had experienced in south Vietnam. Most blacks who were fortunate enough to return alive from Vietnam had been injured mentally, physically, or both. To return and be treated as I had been repeatedly treated by the same U.S. government which I had served as a soldier was unbearable. What had I fought for? Was it all for the white man? To help maintain the white way of life? I thought back to the disproportionate number of Black Americans who fought in Vietnam since many white males had evaded service in Vietnam by obtaining student deferments, joining the National Guard, or having their physicians discover medical conditions that would preclude them from military service. Black men had died in disproportionate numbers on that foreign soil. And in the United States, Blacks had helped build this nation into greatness with our own toil, sweat, tears, with our freedom denied and even at the cost of our own lives. However, whites remained in control and, in my experience, rather than choosing to share control, were trying to keep Black Americans oppressed. Black Americans continued to receive less recognition and remuneration for our efforts. We were not, overall, enjoying the blessings of liberty and the wealth of the United States. A deep heaviness of heart weighed me down.

Also, during this period, I reflected on my father's insistence on my receiving an education. Having studied hard throughout high school, I had the tools to enter college. With higher education, I learned how to submit grant proposals in one of my business classes and had been able to expand my agricultural business into syrup production. My education had enabled me to be more productive, successful, and entrepreneurial. I believe that with my ongoing higher education, I was better able to navigate the USDA and the legal system than Black farmers who had not attended college. Being able to communicate well, both verbally and in written form, is necessary to advance in the modern world. Knowledge, I have learned, is a powerful tool which, when used for good, can break down barriers which have previously hindered progress. With education, my thinking had become more versatile, and I had learned how to fight the system. Without education, I never would have been able to file complaints and make a stand against injustice. I remain thankful for my father's wisdom, and my own in following his wishes. Education has made all the difference, and I do not regret a minute of it.

Chapter 22

Regardless, Serve

Despite the exhaustion from the years fighting for what I knew to be right, and despite sometimes wanting to walk away from it all, I chose to continue to serve my community. God requires us to be faithful to what He calls us to do. The outcomes are in His hands.

Although I had had to curtail some of my physical activity due to my worsening health, I was determined to stay active in my community and to assist my community in any way possible despite the ongoing lawsuits. In 2005, I worked with other local farmers and the State of Alabama's Department of Agriculture and Industries to organize the Greene/Sumter County Farmers' Market. The State held meetings for our farmers, alerting us to the various rules and regulations each farmer would need to follow under Alabama's agricultural guidelines. The Department of Agriculture and Industries also informed us as to what provisions they would extend to citizens who patronized the Greene/Sumter County Farmers' Market. We were delighted to learn that Women, Infant, and Children (WIC) vouchers could be used for fresh produce at our establishment. The State of Alabama provided funding to erect a 100 ft. by 40 – 50 ft. pavilion in Eutaw where we could sell our produce.

In addition to the state's legal requirements, our farmers' market had its own set of rules and regulations for cooperating farmers. As president of the organization, it was my job to ensure all rules were complied with. I also chaired our regular meetings and submitted proposals and grant requests. Some of the development grants we received included the Resource Conservation and Development (RC & D) Council Rural Community grant for the purchase of market coolers, bathroom facilities, and lighting. Our farmers' market provided many services for our members. We provided them a local place of business on Saturday mornings for better marketing of our products to consumers than if we depended on customers to drive out to each of our farms. We were able to acquire bulk rates for fertilizer and lime for members of our cooperative through the Federation of Southern States Co-op. In so doing, we helped members save money too.

Even after the lawsuit and my diminished ability to farm as I had in the past, I continued to work with the farming community. In December 2007, I was re-elected to the Greene/Sumter County FSA Committee for another three-year term, beginning January 1, 2008.[250] The committee chose me to be its chairman as well. Here was God's hand at work and the result of my faithfulness. This same committee which had discriminated against me and wreaked havoc in my life for a quarter of a century, leading to my joining with other plaintiffs in one of the largest lawsuits against the government in United States history, had selected me as chairman. After years of receiving the worst this agency could dish out to those with the least political power in the farming community, I would provide oversight to those making the decisions and could influence what the less powerful would receive. What a great accomplishment this was! During my tenure, I worked to change the agency's dynamics, and ensured fairness toward all participants. I had stood alone. I had been unpopular. I had been a thorn in the side of those withholding equal treatment to African Americans. I had suffered for my stand. But I had stood, even when the odds were against me, even when it was hard and lonely. And in the end, I rose to a position of influence in which I could ensure that others would be treated fairly.

When I was chairman of the Greene/Sumter FSA Committee, we led outreach programs to farmers to enlighten them regarding what programs were available to them. We encouraged them to sign up to participate in programs lending technical and scientific assistance so their farms would be as productive and financially remunerative as possible. We also encouraged local farmers to avail themselves of FSA loan programs and to disaster relief when appropriate. I believe that I have had a lasting influence upon the FSA Committee and the management of the local office. Since I have left my position as chairman, the County Executive Director who manages the FSA office has consistently administered rules and procedures equally, and employees of the office have followed suit.

Also, in 2007, I, along with other military service men and women who had served the United States military in active duty, organized the Greene County American Legion Post #2007. Many of us who had served together in the National Guard unit desired fellowship and communication with past federal active-duty military veterans. Previously, there had been an American Legion post in the area. However, its membership had been overwhelmingly white, and they had not been welcoming to Black military veterans. Besides, that post was inactive in 2007. We saw a void that needed to be filled. The District Commander who would handle our charter was also a Black American. When we shared Greene County's need for an American Legion post, he was only too happy to assist us. Following protocol, we recruited enough founding members, and the group selected me as their Commander. I have served as commander since 2007 through now, in 2020. In addition to providing social events for members and a sense of camaraderie, the American Legion assists veterans and their dependents in obtaining the benefits to which they are entitled, such as help in job searches, scholarship assistance, and access to financial services.

On February 22, 2008, I retired from the United States Army as a Master Sergeant after 40 years of service to my country.[251] I had served my country honorably, and despite my disappointment with my country's discrimination, I remain a proud American and proud of my military service.

Although I had experienced so much discrimination in my county over the years both in law enforcement and in agriculture, in these later years, many organizations have recognized my achievements and my efforts. On June 20, 2009, I became one of five entrepreneurs from the State of Alabama nominated for the Oliver Robinson Foundation Black Achievers Award. Also, on April 22, 2011, I received an award from the University of Alabama School of Medicine in Tuscaloosa. This award was part of its Rural Medical Scholars Program, and I was honored as an Outstanding Community Partner in Alabama Agromedicine.[252] My niece was a student at the University of Alabama at the time and had delivered a presentation featuring much of my work as chairman for West Alabama Health Services, Inc. and my efforts to create a farmers' market, providing greater access to healthier foods for the local population, including WIC recipients. The school was impressed with the information she had shared and subsequently selected me for the award.

Congresswoman Terri Sewell visited me at my farm on November 2, 2011. She served as my representative to Congress at that time and was working on the agricultural committee. She wanted to discuss issues concerning the 2010 farm bill directly with farmers in her district. My farm was one of five which she toured and visited. We discussed the basic needs of small-scale farmers including the importance of access to farm loans and farm programs.

On June 6, 2012, I was appointed to the Greene County Local Emergency Planning Committee and was selected as Acting Chairman. Then on December 23, 2013, I was appointed to the Greene County Water and Sewer Authority Board and was selected as Secretary of that Board. I remain a member of both organizations to this day in 2020. As a Board member for the Local Emergency Planning Committee, I work with the 9-1-1 call center, FEMA, the American Red Cross, and other organizations that exist to ensure our community is well-prepared for and provided for during times of crisis. As a member of the Water and Sewer Authority Board, I help oversee the water authority employees and the water system supplying Greene County residents with safe drinking water and waste removal.

On Sunday, July 27, 2014, I spoke at our annual Greene County Freedom Day festival at the Eutaw National Guard building, reminding our community of the long hard fight for civil rights. I encouraged our community to talk with our youth, to let them know what life was like and how we fought for life to be different in our country for Black Americans. The Alabama Civil Rights Museum honored me with the Rosa Parks Freedom Award.[253] It was truly an honor! The towns of Eutaw, Boligee, Union, and Forkland, the Greene County Board of Education, the

Greene County Commission, and the Alabama Civil Rights Museum sponsored the event.[254] Rev. Thomas Gilmore of Birmingham was the keynote speaker. Also, there were refreshments and entertainment from gospel choirs and soloists from around the area.[255] I am proud to have made a difference in the struggle for civil rights. My life has not been easy. Would it have been easier if I just bowed my head under the weight of oppression and never stood up for myself? Perhaps. But I was not created that way. My gifts include a deep love for and desire to help my community and an ability to stand up to bullies whether they are individuals or organizations. I hope that my work has made my community a better place to live for everyone. Being honored that day showed me that maybe others thought I had accomplished my mission, and for that I am grateful.

Chapter 23

Reflections

Over the years, I have reflected upon the Black farmers' lawsuit. Knowing what I know now regarding the disappointing outcome of the lawsuit and the extreme financial, emotional, and physical toll it exacted upon me, would I have made the same choices? I believe I would. Despite the gains of the civil rights movement decades before, I had been treated as a second-class citizen in farming. This mistreatment, as I learned during this process, was widespread. In a sense, I faced a moral obligation to stand up for myself and the many other Black farmers who could not stand up for themselves. If I did not make a stand, if I and my fellow plaintiffs did not draw national attention to the deeply ingrained racial prejudice and discrimination in the USDA and its local FSA offices, the mistreatment would continue. I also believe I made a good decision in reaching a settlement when I did. Neither I nor the other lead plaintiffs in the Pigford v. Glickman lawsuit had the resources to continue fighting against the federal government. I must see my work as part of a larger and ongoing effort to secure the blessings of liberty for our posterity, as the U.S. Constitution which I have fought to defend declares. Nevertheless, the hurt lingers.

In my life, I have found that we are interdependent. I am grateful to those who came before me and braved injustice to give me life and the ability to fight for my rights. Many others have fought for the rights of African Americans along with me. Some are famous, but most, like me, are not. I surely did not achieve everything on my own. I needed support from other sources, from friends and family, from the larger community, and of course from God. I hope that I in turn have paved the way for an easier life with less discrimination and injustice for those who come after me.

Many who have witnessed the trials I have faced have wondered how I survived all I have been through. Throughout all my trials, I have depended on the Lord. That has been the key. The Serenity Prayer by Reinhold Niebuhr has had a profound impact upon me. "God, grant me the serenity to accept the things I cannot change; courage to change the things I can; and wisdom to know the difference." If not for the courage with which the Lord emboldened me, I would not have been able to face all the obstacles life and racially unjust systems had placed in my way. I know I cannot change anyone's heart. Only God can do that, and He allows events to unfold as He chooses for the ultimate good of all. At no point could I make things or people around me change, and I have depended heavily upon the Lord in all the battles I have faced, especially those of racial injustice and inequality. I know God wants His will accomplished on earth just as it is in Heaven, and if He wanted me to help bring that about in some small way by shining light upon the darkness of injustice around me, then I am honored to have been in His service. Others rendered this service for me, and it is fitting and right for me to do the same for those coming after me.

Another insight I have had as I look back upon my life is that some things that were meant for evil turn out to be good for us. Again and again, the Lord has proven Himself faithful to His promise in Romans 8:28, "And we know that all things work together for good to them that love God, to them who are called according to His purpose." While it hurt terribly to lose my re-election bid for sheriff in 1999, for example, in the end I found that God's hand was in this also. The office had been the source of a great deal of stress, and there were more battles I would face which would need my full attention. Losing the election was better for my health. Repeatedly, I have found that the very things that were intended to tear me down only served to make me stronger in the long run. What man had meant for evil, God turned to good.

My advice today for a younger generation of African Americans is not to take anything for granted. Develop a strong moral and spiritual foundation. Community matters. We must stand together and remember how interconnected we are and how we need and depend on one another. In the past, dependence upon one another was a matter of survival. However, in the past couple generations, our society has become increasingly individualistic. I think that this separates us and weakens us. It really does take a community to raise a child. We need to think about our responsibility to the broader community and not just about what is best for ourselves. Yet today, we do not have the same need to work together. Families are more separated from each other, and individuals seem intent on doing things their own way and for their own benefit. The only way to move forward is to do so together.

Also, education matters. Without an education, I never would have developed the tools to fight systemic injustice. Learn history. Learn civics. Learn about business and electronics and computers. Learn basic self-sufficiency skills. Learn to communicate effectively. Learn everything you can. With these tools we can achieve amazing results.

I am an American. I am an African American. I am a veteran. I have fought for the United States abroad, and I have fought for our principles here at home. I have believed that we could and should be better than we have been. In my lifetime, I have seen real progress. African Americans can vote and hold jobs that were never an option for us before. African Americans have more of a voice in our culture. It takes time to change, to move forward, but we have made positive strides. Yet, I still have heartburn when I see ongoing discrimination. Oh, it is more hidden now, but it remains. We made some progress with more representation in local and national politics. But in 2016, the nation elected a president who appears to sow division, and racial tensions appear on the rise again. Clearly, he did not create these tensions, but they seem more out in the open. For example, as an American, an African American, a veteran, a Christian, and a former law enforcement officer, I respected Colin Kaepernick for taking a knee to stand against injustice against African Americans. He tried peacefully and respectfully to draw national attention to a systemic issue. He challenged us to do better, one of the most American things an American can do. And yet, a man with no military experience, who never fought for our country took offense and called him obscene names. It is difficult for me to watch us stumbling backwards after all I marched, fought, and advocated for for decades now. My hope remains in God that we will not succumb to renewed racist attitudes and injustice. We will overcome. May God have mercy upon us.

Co-Author's Note

Tenacious: One Man's Lifelong Struggle for Racial Justice is part memoir, part autobiography, and part compilation of oral history. George Hall fearlessly and tenaciously stood against racial discrimination throughout his life, culminating in the Pigford v. Glickman (1999) lawsuit, and he wanted to tell his story. Unfortunately, shortly after beginning our project, COVID-19 hit the United States, severely limiting safe travel between our homes. However, the two of us spent many hours conversing over the phone and via email. While it is often difficult to substantiate claims or to recreate a timeline from memory, Mr. Hall kept many records of correspondence, complaint filings, and official reports— he kept the receipts—and he shared what he could with me. Mr. Hall also shared with me a prior short version of many of his recollections that he had compiled over the years in hopes that it would serve as a foundation for the book which you now hold in your hands. These documents were invaluable in fleshing out his recollections in greater detail. In addition, I delved into the historical context of racial discrimination, Jim Crow, and the Civil Rights Movement to add to the framework and setting of his story. We discussed at length this history of the United States, which was in fact Mr. Hall's lived experience, and how he was personally affected by the racism endemic in American culture.

Tenacious is, by its nature as a memoir, a personal account. However, when added to the voices of many others, it paints a picture of the struggles of many African Americans like George Hall in the second half of the twentieth century in the United States. Since memory by nature can be imperfect, we have relied upon and cited numerous external resources, providing corroboration for Mr. Hall's lived experience, which also add important historical detail to the setting of his story. Mr. Hall and I also opted to use specific names of individuals primarily when they seemed important in the telling of his story and when easily discoverable via external documentation. We also acknowledge and respect that others may have experienced these same events from different perspectives, and therefore may remember them differently. In fact, historians must regularly sift through the differing perspectives in the historical records to add depth to our knowledge of the past.

My hope as a student of U.S. history is that <u>Tenacious</u> will provide yet another first-person perspective for future historians who wish to continue studying the Pigford v. Glickman lawsuit and racial discrimination in the U.S. agricultural industry. I also hope researchers will avail themselves of the extensive collection of George Hall's papers, now housed at the Alabama Department of Archives and History.

Working on this project with Mr. Hall has been a great honor. A friend told me about Mr. Hall and his involvement in Pigford v. Glickman. After meeting him and hearing more about his life and experiences, I agreed that people needed to hear his story, and so our work together began. I hope others will be inspired by Mr. Hall to speak out about injustices they witness or experience and, in doing so, continue to inch the United States towards our national aspiration to become a more perfect union, with liberty and justice for all.

- L.R.T.

Endnotes

CHAPTER 2

[1] Hansan, J.E. (2011). "Jim Crow laws and racial segregation." Social Welfare History Project. Retrieved on January 11, 2020 from https://socialwelfare.library.vcu.edu/eras/civil-war-reconstruction/jim-crow-laws-andracial-segregation/

[2] Stevenson, Bryan, et. al. (2017) "Lynching in America: Confronting the Legacy of Racial Terror (Report) (3rd Edition)." *Equal Justice Initiative.* Montgomery, Alabama: Retrieved January 11, 2020 from https://lynchinginamerica.eji.org/report/

[3] Williams, Jasmine K. (Feb. 14, 2006). "The Plague of Jim Crow." *The New York Post.* Retrieved January 28, 2020 from https://nypost.com/2006/02/14/the-plague-of-jim-crow/

[4] "The Civil Rights Act of 1964." *Constitutional Rights Foundation.* Retrieved January 28, 2020 from https://www.crf-usa.org/black-history-month/the-civil-rights-act-of-1964

[5] Duignan, B. (March 9, 2020). "Plessy v. Ferguson: Law Case [1896]." *Encyclopaedia Britannica.* Retrieved January 11, 2020 from https://www.britannica.com/event/Plessy-v-Ferguson-1896

[6] Kendi, I. X., (2016). "Stamped from the Beginning." (p. 362). New York City, New York. Nation Books.

[7] "The 'Southern Manifesto' 102 Cong. Rec. 4515-16 (1956)." *University of Utah College of Behavioral and Social Science.* Retrieved on March 31, 2020 from

http://content.csbs.utah.edu/~dlevin/federalism/southern_manifesto.html

[8] "Browder v. Gayle, 352 U.S. 903." *Stanford University: The Martin Luther King, Jr. Research and Education Institute.* Retrieved on January 11, 2020 from https://kinginstitute.stanford.edu/encyclopedia/browder-v-gayle-352-us-903

[9] "The Montgomery Bus Boycott." *Stanford University: The Martin Luther King, Jr. Research and Education Institute.* Retrieved on January 11, 2020 from https://kinginstitute.stanford.edu/encyclopedia/montgomery-bus-boycott

CHAPTER 3

[10] "What is Agent Orange?" *The Aspen Institute.* Retrieved on January 29, 2020 from https://www.aspeninstitute.org/programs/agent-orange-in-vietnam-program/what-is-agent-orange/
[11] "What is Agent Orange?" *The Aspen Institute.* Retrieved on January 29, 2020 from https://www.aspeninstitute.org/programs/agent-orange-in-vietnam-program/what-is-agent-orange/

CHAPTER 4

[12] Taylor, S. N. and J. D. Santoro. (Online December 14, 2018. doi: 10.7759/cureus.3733)"Racial Bias in the US Opioid Epidemic: A Review of the History of Systemic Bias and Implications for Care." *Cureus.* Retrieved on January 29, 2020 from https://www.ncbi.nlm.nih.gov/pmc/articles/PMC6384031/

CHAPTER 5

[13] (March 30, 1972.) "Alabama Appoints First Three Blacks As State Troopers." *The New York Times.* Retrieved on January 29, 2020 from https://www.nytimes.com/1972/03/30/archives/alabama-appoints-first-three-blacks-as-state-troopers.html

[14] Tyler, S. S., and E. Moore. (2013). "Plight of Black Farmers in the Context of USDA Farm Loan Programs: A Research Agenda for the Future." *Professional Agricultural Workers Journal.* Retrieved on February 5, 2020 from http://ageconsearch.umn.edu/record/236726/files/Shakara%20S.%20Tyler.pdf

[15] Thurow, R. (Updated May 1, 1998.) "Black Farmers Plow the Path To Washington Seeking Paydirt." *The Wall Street Journal.* Retrieved on January 23, 2020 from https://www.wsj.com/articles/SB893900013990577500

CHAPTER 7

[16] EEOC Complaint filed in Birmingham District on February 7, 1985 by George Hall.

[17] EEOC Complaint filed in Birmingham District on February 7, 1985 by George Hall.

[18] EEOC Complaint filed in Birmingham District on February 7, 1985 by George Hall.

CHAPTER 8

[19] Chandler, F. What are the differences in ribbon cane and sugar cane syrup? Retrieved on July 23, 2020 from https://www.leaf.tv/articles/what-are-the-differences-in-ribbon-cane-sugar-cane-syrup/

[20] Chandler, F. What are the differences in ribbon cane and sugar cane syrup? Retrieved on July 23, 2020 from https://www.leaf.tv/articles/what-are-the-differences-in-ribbon-cane-sugar-cane-syrup/

[21] Reid, D. A. and E. P. Bennett. (2012). "Beyond 40 Acres and a Mule: African American landowning families since Reconstruction." (p. 272). Gainesville, Florida. University Press of Florida.

[22] Gilbert, J., S. D. Wood, and G. Sharp. (2002). "Who Owns the Land? Agricultural Land Ownership." *Rural American*, Volume 17 Issue 4. Retrieved on   from https://web.archive.org/web/20130628135832/http://www.ers.usda.gov/media/562463/ra174h_1_.pdf

[23] "Earl Lauer Butz: American Economist and Government Official." *Encyclopaedia Britannica.* Retrieved on March 31, 2020 from https://www.britannica.com/biography/Earl-Lauer-Butz

[24] Johnson, R. (October 8, 2019.) "We must reject the 'go big or go home' mentality of modern agriculture." *The Hill.* Retrieved on March 31, 2020 from https://thehill.com/opinion/finance/464856-

we-must-reject-the-go-big-or-go-home-mentality-of-modern-agriculture

CHAPTER 9

[25] George Hall to U.S. Representative Earl Hilliard on March 15, 1993 (Letter).

[26] George Hall to U.S. Representative Earl Hilliard on March 15, 1993 (Letter).

[27] George Hall to U.S. Representative Earl Hilliard on March 15, 1993 (Letter).

[28] George Hall to U.S. Representative Earl Hilliard on March 15, 1993 (Letter).

[29] George Hall to U.S. Representative Earl Hilliard on March 15, 1993 (Letter).

[30] George Hall to U.S. Representative Earl Hilliard on March 15, 1993 (Letter).

[30] Romans 8:28; Genesis 50:20

CHAPTER 10

[32] "Federally Qualified Health Centers (FQHCs) and the Health Center Program." *Rural Health Information Hub.* Retrieved on March 31, 2020 from https://www.ruralhealthinfo.org/topics/federally-qualified-health-centers

[33] Iris Sermon (2020). Interviewed by L. R. Turochy February 6.

[34] Iris Sermon (2020). Interviewed by L. R. Turochy February 6.

[35] Iris Sermon (2020). Interviewed by L. R. Turochy February 6.

[36] Iris Sermon (2020). Interviewed by L. R. Turochy February 6.

[37] Iris Sermon (2020). Interviewed by L. R. Turochy February 6.

[38] Iris Sermon (2020). Interviewed by L. R. Turochy February 6.

[39] Iris Sermon (2020). Interviewed by L. R. Turochy February 6.

[40] Iris Sermon (2020). Interviewed by L. R. Turochy February 6.

[41] Iris Sermon (2020). Interviewed by L. R. Turochy February 6.

[42] Iris Sermon (2020). Interviewed by L. R. Turochy February 6.

[43] Iris Sermon (2020). Interviewed by L. R. Turochy February 6.

[44] Iris Sermon (2020). Interviewed by L. R. Turochy February 6.

[45] Iris Sermon (2020). Interviewed by L. R. Turochy February 6.

[46] Iris Sermon (2020). Interviewed by L. R. Turochy February 6.

[47] Iris Sermon (2020). Interviewed by L. R. Turochy February 6.

CHAPTER 11

[48] Stillman College Bachelor of Arts diploma conferred upon George W. Hall on May 7, 1994.

[49] "The Sweet Taste of Success". Article excerpt (photocopied), source unknown.

[50] "The Sweet Taste of Success". Article excerpt (photocopied), source unknown.

[51] "The Sweet Taste of Success". Article excerpt (photocopied), source unknown.

[52] "The Sweet Taste of Success". Article excerpt (photocopied), source unknown.

[53] 52nd Annual Professional Agricultural Workers Conference. Tuskegee University. L.A. Potts Success Story "The Sweet Taste of Success". Presented to George Hall in Eutaw, AL. on Dec. 5, 1994. (Award)

[54] USDA Civil Rights Operations Program Complaint Final Decision. Case Number 950420. Wardell C. Townsend, Jr. Asst. Secretary for Administration. August 9, 1996.

[55] USDA Civil Rights Operations Program Complaint Final Decision. Case Number 950420. Wardell C. Townsend, Jr. Asst. Secretary for Administration. August 9, 1996.

[56] USDA Civil Rights Operations Program Complaint Final Decision. Case Number 950420. Wardell C. Townsend, Jr. Asst. Secretary for Administration. August 9, 1996.

[57] George Hall of Hall's Farm to Mr. Montoya, Director Office of Civil Rights USDA on April 20, 1995 (Letter).

[58] George Hall of Hall's Farm to Mr. Montoya, Director Office of Civil Rights USDA on April 20, 1995 (Letter).

[59] John W. Dumas, USDA, to Barbara Nelson, EEO and Civil Rights Staff, USDA on October 2, 1995 (Letter).

[60] John W. Dumas, USDA, to Barbara Nelson, EEO and Civil Rights Staff, USDA on October 2, 1995 (Letter).

[61] USDA Civil Rights Operations Program Complaint Final Decision. Case Number 950420. Wardell C. Townsend, Jr. Asst. Secretary for Administration. August 9, 1996.

[62] (September 4, 1996.) "Lashley, McGee removed from FSA Committee for discrimination." *The Democrat (Greene Co., AL).*

[63] George Hall of Hall's Farm to Mr. Montoya, Director Office of Civil Rights USDA on April 20, 1995 (Letter).

[64] George Hall of Hall's Farm to Mr. Montoya, Director Office of Civil Rights USDA on April 20, 1995 (Letter).

[65] George Hall of Hall's Farm to Mr. Montoya, Director Office of Civil Rights USDA on April 20, 1995 (Letter).

[66] George Hall of Hall's Farm to Mr. Montoya, Director Office of Civil Rights USDA on April 20, 1995 (Letter).

[67] John W. Dumas, USDA, to Barbara Nelson, EEO and Civil Rights Staff, USDA on October 2, 1995 (Letter).

[68] John W. Dumas, USDA, to Barbara Nelson, EEO and Civil Rights Staff, USDA on October 2, 1995 (Letter).

[69] John W. Dumas, USDA, to Barbara Nelson, EEO and Civil Rights Staff, USDA on October 2, 1995 (Letter).

[70] John W. Dumas, USDA, to Barbara Nelson, EEO and Civil Rights Staff, USDA on October 2, 1995 (Letter).

[71] John W. Dumas, USDA, to Barbara Nelson, EEO and Civil Rights Staff, USDA on October 2, 1995 (Letter).

[72] John W. Dumas, USDA, to Barbara Nelson, EEO and Civil Rights Staff, USDA on October 2, 1995 (Letter).

[73] John W. Dumas, USDA, to Barbara Nelson, EEO and Civil Rights Staff, USDA on October 2, 1995 (Letter).

[74] John W. Dumas, USDA, to Barbara Nelson, EEO and Civil Rights Staff, USDA on October 2, 1995 (Letter).

[75] John W. Dumas, USDA, to Barbara Nelson, EEO and Civil Rights Staff, USDA on October 2, 1995 (Letter).

CHAPTER 12

[76] Walton, V. (January 13, 1996.) "Black Churches Burn in Boligee." *Birmingham News (AL)*. Retrieved on January 28, 2020 from https://drive.google.com/file/d/0B-BE8fl6oNWaOFhhby1hQkNLcXM/view

[77] Walton, V. (January 13, 1996.) "Black Churches Burn in Boligee." *Birmingham News (AL)*. Retrieved on January 28, 2020 from https://drive.google.com/file/d/0B-BE8fl6oNWaOFhhby1hQkNLcXM/view

[78] Walton, V. (January 13, 1996.) "Black Churches Burn in Boligee." *Birmingham News (AL)*. Retrieved on January 28, 2020 from

https://drive.google.com/file/d/0B-
BE8fl6oNWaOFhhby1hQkNLcXM/view

[79] Press, R. (August 5, 1996.) *"A Town with Two of Everything."* The
*Christian Science Monitor. Retrieved on January 28, 2020 from
https://www.csmonitor.com/1996/0805/080596.feat.cover.1.html*

[80] Press, R. (August 5, 1996.) *"A Town with Two of Everything."* The
*Christian Science Monitor. Retrieved on January 28, 2020 from
https://www.csmonitor.com/1996/0805/080596.feat.cover.1.html*

[81] Press, R. (August 5, 1996.) *"A Town with Two of Everything."* The
*Christian Science Monitor. Retrieved on January 28, 2020 from
https://www.csmonitor.com/1996/0805/080596.feat.cover.1.html*

[82] Press, R. (August 5, 1996.) *"A Town with Two of Everything."* The
*Christian Science Monitor. Retrieved on January 28, 2020 from
https://www.csmonitor.com/1996/0805/080596.feat.cover.1.html*

[83] Press, R. (August 5, 1996.) *"A Town with Two of Everything."* The
*Christian Science Monitor. Retrieved on January 28, 2020 from
https://www.csmonitor.com/1996/0805/080596.feat.cover.1.html*

[84] Press, R. (August 5, 1996.) *"A Town with Two of Everything."* The
*Christian Science Monitor. Retrieved on January 28, 2020 from
https://www.csmonitor.com/1996/0805/080596.feat.cover.1.html*

[85] Press, R. (August 5, 1996.) *"A Town with Two of Everything."* The
*Christian Science Monitor. Retrieved on January 28, 2020 from
https://www.csmonitor.com/1996/0805/080596.feat.cover.1.html*

[86] Transcript of Alabama Advisory Committee to the U.S.
Commission on Civil Rights, Community Forum held June 26, 1997
in Boligee Alabama

[87] Transcript of Alabama Advisory Committee to the U.S. Commission on Civil Rights, Community Forum held June 26, 1997 in Boligee Alabama

[88] Transcript of Alabama Advisory Committee to the U.S. Commission on Civil Rights, Community Forum held June 26, 1997 in Boligee Alabama

[89] Transcript of Alabama Advisory Committee to the U.S. Commission on Civil Rights, Community Forum held June 26, 1997 in Boligee Alabama

CHAPTER 13

[90] USDA Civil Rights Operations Program Complaint Final Decision. Case Number 950420. Wardell C. Townsend, Jr. Asst. Secretary for Administration. August 9, 1996.

[91] USDA Civil Rights Operations Program Complaint Final Decision. Case Number 950420. Wardell C. Townsend, Jr. Asst. Secretary for Administration. August 9, 1996.

[92] USDA Civil Rights Operations Program Complaint Final Decision. Case Number 950420. Wardell C. Townsend, Jr. Asst. Secretary for Administration. August 9, 1996.

[93] USDA Civil Rights Operations Program Complaint Final Decision. Case Number 950420. Wardell C. Townsend, Jr. Asst. Secretary for Administration. August 9, 1996.

[94] USDA Civil Rights Operations Program Complaint Final Decision. Case Number 950420. Wardell C. Townsend, Jr. Asst. Secretary for Administration. August 9, 1996.

[95] USDA Civil Rights Operations Program Complaint Final Decision. Case Number 950420. Wardell C. Townsend, Jr. Asst. Secretary for Administration. August 9, 1996.

[96] USDA Civil Rights Operations Program Complaint Final Decision. Case Number 950420. Wardell C. Townsend, Jr. Asst. Secretary for Administration. August 9, 1996.

[97] USDA Civil Rights Operations Program Complaint Final Decision. Case Number 950420. Wardell C. Townsend, Jr. Asst. Secretary for Administration. August 9, 1996.

[98] USDA Civil Rights Operations Program Complaint Final Decision. Case Number 950420. Wardell C. Townsend, Jr. Asst. Secretary for Administration. August 9, 1996.

[99] USDA Civil Rights Operations Program Complaint Final Decision. Case Number 950420. Wardell C. Townsend, Jr. Asst. Secretary for Administration. August 9, 1996.

[100] USDA Civil Rights Operations Program Complaint Final Decision. Case Number 950420. Wardell C. Townsend, Jr. Asst. Secretary for Administration. August 9, 1996.

[101] (September 4, 1996.) "Lashley, McGee removed from FSA Committee for discrimination." *The Democrat (Greene Co., AL).*

[102] (September 4, 1996.) "Lashley, McGee removed from FSA Committee for discrimination." *The Democrat (Greene Co., AL).*

[103] (September 4, 1996.) "Lashley, McGee removed from FSA Committee for discrimination." *The Democrat (Greene Co., AL).*

[104] (September 4, 1996.) "Lashley, McGee removed from FSA Committee for discrimination." *The Democrat (Greene Co., AL).*

CHAPTER 15

[105] Thurow, R. (Updated May 1, 1998.) "Black Farmers Plow the Path To Washington Seeking Paydirt." *The Wall Street Journal.* Retrieved on January 23, 2020 from https://www.wsj.com/articles/SB893900013990577500

[106] Thurow, R. (Updated May 1, 1998.) "Black Farmers Plow the Path To Washington Seeking Paydirt." *The Wall Street Journal.* Retrieved on January 23, 2020 from https://www.wsj.com/articles/SB893900013990577500

[107] Thurow, R. (Updated May 1, 1998.) "Black Farmers Plow the Path To Washington Seeking Paydirt." *The Wall Street Journal.* Retrieved on January 23, 2020 from https://www.wsj.com/articles/SB893900013990577500

[108] Thurow, R. (Updated May 1, 1998.) "Black Farmers Plow the Path To Washington Seeking Paydirt." *The Wall Street Journal.* Retrieved on January 23, 2020 from https://www.wsj.com/articles/SB893900013990577500

[109] Thurow, R. (Updated May 1, 1998.) "Black Farmers Plow the Path To Washington Seeking Paydirt." *The Wall Street Journal.* Retrieved on January 23, 2020 from https://www.wsj.com/articles/SB893900013990577500

[110] Thurow, R. (Updated May 1, 1998.) "Black Farmers Plow the Path To Washington Seeking Paydirt." *The Wall Street Journal.* Retrieved on January 23, 2020 from https://www.wsj.com/articles/SB893900013990577500

[111] Thurow, R. (Updated May 1, 1998.) "Black Farmers Plow the Path To Washington Seeking Paydirt." *The Wall Street Journal.* Retrieved on January 23, 2020 from https://www.wsj.com/articles/SB893900013990577500

[112] Thurow, R. (Updated May 1, 1998.) "Black Farmers Plow the Path To Washington Seeking Paydirt." *The Wall Street Journal.* Retrieved on January 23, 2020 from https://www.wsj.com/articles/SB893900013990577500

[113] Thurow, R. (Updated May 1, 1998.) "Black Farmers Plow the Path To Washington Seeking Paydirt." *The Wall Street Journal.* Retrieved on January 23, 2020 from https://www.wsj.com/articles/SB893900013990577500

[114] Thurow, R. (Updated May 1, 1998.) "Black Farmers Plow the Path To Washington Seeking Paydirt." *The Wall Street Journal.* Retrieved on January 23, 2020 from https://www.wsj.com/articles/SB893900013990577500

[115] Thurow, R. (Updated May 1, 1998.) "Black Farmers Plow the Path To Washington Seeking Paydirt." *The Wall Street Journal.* Retrieved on January 23, 2020 from https://www.wsj.com/articles/SB893900013990577500

[116] Thurow, R. (Updated May 1, 1998.) "Black Farmers Plow the Path To Washington Seeking Paydirt." *The Wall Street Journal.* Retrieved on January 23, 2020 from https://www.wsj.com/articles/SB893900013990577500

[117] Thurow, R. (Updated May 1, 1998.) "Black Farmers Plow the Path To Washington Seeking Paydirt." *The Wall Street Journal.* Retrieved on January 23, 2020 from https://www.wsj.com/articles/SB893900013990577500

[118] Thurow, R. (Updated May 1, 1998.) "Black Farmers Plow the Path To Washington Seeking Paydirt." *The Wall Street Journal.* Retrieved on January 23, 2020 from https://www.wsj.com/articles/SB893900013990577500

[119] Thurow, R. (Updated May 1, 1998.) "Black Farmers Plow the Path To Washington Seeking Paydirt." *The Wall Street Journal.* Retrieved on January 23, 2020 from https://www.wsj.com/articles/SB893900013990577500

[120] Thurow, R. (Updated May 1, 1998.) "Black Farmers Plow the Path To Washington Seeking Paydirt." *The Wall Street Journal.* Retrieved on January 23, 2020 from https://www.wsj.com/articles/SB893900013990577500

[121] Thurow, R. (Updated May 1, 1998.) USDA Civil Rights Operations Program Complaint Final Decision. Case Number 950420. Wardell C. Townsend, Jr. Asst. Secretary for Administration. August 9, 1996.
The Wall Street Journal. Retrieved on January 23, 2020 from https://www.wsj.com/articles/SB893900013990577500

[122] "Notice of Class Certification and Proposed Class Settlement." Civil Action No 97-1978. Retrieved on February 26, 2020 from https://www.dm.usda.gov/pigford.pdf

[123] "Notice of Class Certification and Proposed Class Settlement." Civil Action No 97-1978. Retrieved on February 26, 2020 from https://www.dm.usda.gov/pigford.pdf

[124] Cowan, T. and J. Feder. (May 29, 2013.) "The Pigford Cases: USDA Settlement of Discrimination Suits by Black Farmers." *Congressional Research Service Report for Congress.* Retrieved on

February 27, 2020 from https://nationalaglawcenter.org/wp-content/uploads/assets/crs/RS20430.pdf

[125] "Notice of Class Certification and Proposed Class Settlement." Civil Action No 97-1978. Retrieved on February 26, 2020 from https://www.dm.usda.gov/pigford.pdf

[126] Thurow, R. (Updated May 1, 1998.) "Black Farmers Plow the Path To Washington Seeking Paydirt." *The Wall Street Journal.* Retrieved on January 23, 2020 from https://www.wsj.com/articles/SB893900013990577500

[127] Thurow, R. (Updated May 1, 1998.) "Black Farmers Plow the Path To Washington Seeking Paydirt." *The Wall Street Journal.* Retrieved on January 23, 2020 from https://www.wsj.com/articles/SB893900013990577500

[128] (July 20, 2004.) "A Century of USDA's Institutionalized Racism Subjects African American Farmers to Dramatic Land Loss." *Environmental Working Group.* Retrieved on February 26, 2020 from https://www.ewg.org/research/obstruction-justice/century-usdas-institutionalized-racism-subjects-african-american

[129] (July 20, 2004.) "A Century of USDA's Institutionalized Racism Subjects African American Farmers to Dramatic Land Loss." *Environmental Working Group.* Retrieved on February 26, 2020 from https://www.ewg.org/research/obstruction-justice/century-usdas-institutionalized-racism-subjects-african-american

[130] Thurow, R. (Updated May 1, 1998.) "Black Farmers Plow the Path To Washington Seeking Paydirt." *The Wall Street Journal.* Retrieved on January 23, 2020 from https://www.wsj.com/articles/SB893900013990577500

[131] Gill, R. (2017.) "Pearlie Sylvester Reed (1948- 2016)." Encyclopedia of Arkansas. Retrieved on February 26, 2020 from https://encyclopediaofarkansas.net/entries/pearlie-sylvester-reed-8235/

[132] (February 27, 1997.) "Report for the Secretary on Civil Rights Issues-Phase I" Retrieved on February 26, 2020 from https://www.usda.gov/oig/webdocs/oig.htm

[133] (February 27, 1997.) "Report for the Secretary on Civil Rights Issues-Phase I" Retrieved on February 26, 2020 from https://www.usda.gov/oig/webdocs/oig.htm

CHAPTER 16

[134] Cowan, T. and J. Feder. (May 29, 2013.) "The Pigford Cases: USDA Settlement of Discrimination Suits by Black Farmers." *Congressional Research Service Report for Congress.* Retrieved on February 27, 2020 from https://nationalaglawcenter.org/wp-content/uploads/assets/crs/RS20430.pdf

[135] Cowan, T. and J. Feder. (May 29, 2013.) "The Pigford Cases: USDA Settlement of Discrimination Suits by Black Farmers." *Congressional Research Service Report for Congress.* Retrieved on February 27, 2020 from https://nationalaglawcenter.org/wp-content/uploads/assets/crs/RS20430.pdf

[136] Cowan, T. and J. Feder. (May 29, 2013.) "The Pigford Cases: USDA Settlement of Discrimination Suits by Black Farmers." *Congressional Research Service Report for Congress.* Retrieved on February 27, 2020 from https://nationalaglawcenter.org/wp-content/uploads/assets/crs/RS20430.pdf

[137] Cowan, T. and J. Feder. (May 29, 2013.) "The Pigford Cases: USDA Settlement of Discrimination Suits by Black Farmers."

Congressional Research Service Report for Congress. Retrieved on February 27, 2020 from https://nationalaglawcenter.org/wp-content/uploads/assets/crs/RS20430.pdf

[138] Cowan, T. and J. Feder. (May 29, 2013.) "The Pigford Cases: USDA Settlement of Discrimination Suits by Black Farmers." *Congressional Research Service Report for Congress.* Retrieved on February 27, 2020 from https://nationalaglawcenter.org/wp-content/uploads/assets/crs/RS20430.pdf

[139] Cowan, T. and J. Feder. (May 29, 2013.) "The Pigford Cases: USDA Settlement of Discrimination Suits by Black Farmers." *Congressional Research Service Report for Congress.* Retrieved on February 27, 2020 from https://nationalaglawcenter.org/wp-content/uploads/assets/crs/RS20430.pdf

[140] Cowan, T. and J. Feder. (May 29, 2013.) "The Pigford Cases: USDA Settlement of Discrimination Suits by Black Farmers." *Congressional Research Service Report for Congress.* Retrieved on February 27, 2020 from https://nationalaglawcenter.org/wp-content/uploads/assets/crs/RS20430.pdf

[141] Castro, A. and Z. Willingham. (April 3, 2019.) "Progressive Governance Can Turn the Tide for Black Farmers." *Center for American Progress.* Retrieved on February 27, 2020 from https://www.americanprogress.org/issues/economy/reports/2019/04/03/467892/progressive-governance-can-turn-tide-black-farmers/

[142] (2018.) "*In re Black Farmers Discrimination Litigation,* Case 1:08-mc-00511-PLF, Document 500, in the U.S. District Court for the District of Columbia." Retrieved on February 27, 2020 from https://www.blackfarmercase.com/Documents/BFDL%20-

%20Order%20re%20Phase%20I%20Cy%20Pres%20Beneficiaries%201.10.17.pdf

[143] Cowan, T. and J. Feder. (May 29, 2013.) "The Pigford Cases: USDA Settlement of Discrimination Suits by Black Farmers." *Congressional Research Service Report for Congress.* Retrieved on February 27, 2020 from https://nationalaglawcenter.org/wp-content/uploads/assets/crs/RS20430.pdf

[144] Cowan, T. and J. Feder. (May 29, 2013.) "The Pigford Cases: USDA Settlement of Discrimination Suits by Black Farmers." *Congressional Research Service Report for Congress.* Retrieved on February 27, 2020 from https://nationalaglawcenter.org/wp-content/uploads/assets/crs/RS20430.pdf

[145] Pigford v Glickman (1999) Agreement to Resolve Claims of George Hall on April 15, 1999 from personal records.

[146] Pigford v Glickman (1999) Agreement to Resolve Claims of George Hall on April 15, 1999 from personal records.

[147] Pigford v Glickman (1999) Agreement to Resolve Claims of George Hall on April 15, 1999 from personal records.

CHAPTER 17

[148] "First President of the Tuskegee University Cooperative Extension Program Advisory Council". Tuskegee University Cooperative Extension Program. Certificate of Appreciation. Presented to George Hall on Feb. 13, 1998. (Award)

[149] "For Services Rendered to the Community". Heifer Project International. Golden Achievement Award. Presented to George Hall on August 13, 1998. (Award)

[150] T. M. Campbell Leadership Award. Tuskegee University Cooperative Extension Program. Presented to George Hall in Eutaw, AL on February 11, 1999. (Award).

[151] George Hall of Hall's Farm to Honorable Ann Veneman Secretary of Agriculture on October 22, 2001 (Letter).

[152] George Hall of Hall's Farm to Honorable Ann Veneman Secretary of Agriculture on October 22, 2001 (Letter).

[153] George Hall of Hall's Farm to Honorable Ann Veneman Secretary of Agriculture on October 22, 2001 (Letter).

[154] George Hall of Hall's Farm to Honorable Ann Veneman Secretary of Agriculture on October 22, 2001 (Letter).

[155] George Hall of Hall's Farm to Honorable Ann Veneman Secretary of Agriculture on October 22, 2001 (Letter).

[156] USDA Office of the Secretary National Appeals Division Appeal Determination Case No. 2002S001180 November 7, 2002.

[157] George Hall of Hall's Farm to Honorable Ann Veneman Secretary of Agriculture on October 22, 2001 (Letter).

[158] George Hall of Hall's Farm to Honorable Ann Veneman Secretary of Agriculture on October 22, 2001 (Letter).

[159] George Hall of Hall's Farm to Honorable Ann Veneman Secretary of Agriculture on October 22, 2001 (Letter).

[160] George Hall of Hall's Farm to Honorable Ann Veneman Secretary of Agriculture on October 22, 2001 (Letter).

[161] George Hall of Hall's Farm to Honorable Ann Veneman Secretary of Agriculture on October 22, 2001 (Letter).

[162] George Hall of Hall's Farm to Honorable Ann Veneman Secretary of Agriculture on October 22, 2001 (Letter).

[163] George Hall of Hall's Farm to Honorable Ann Veneman Secretary of Agriculture on October 22, 2001 (Letter).

[164] Memorandum Opinion and Order United States Court of Federal Claims No. 05-517C Filed October 31, 2005. Retrieved from https://casetext.com/case/hall-v-us-49 on July 27, 2020.

[165] USDA Office of the Secretary National Appeals Division Appeal Determination Case No. 2002S001180 November 7, 2002.

[166] USDA Office of the Secretary National Appeals Division Appeal Determination Case No. 2002S001180 November 7, 2002.

[167] USDA Office of the Secretary National Appeals Division Appeal Determination Case No. 2002S001180 November 7, 2002.

[168] USDA Office of the Secretary National Appeals Division Appeal Determination Case No. 2002S001180 November 7, 2002.

[169] USDA Office of the Secretary National Appeals Division Appeal Determination Case No. 2002S001180 November 7, 2002.

[170] George Hall of Hall's Farm to Honorable Ann Veneman Secretary of Agriculture on January 29, 2003 (Letter).

[171] George Hall of Hall's Farm to Honorable Ann Veneman Secretary of Agriculture on January 29, 2003 (Letter).

[172] George Hall of Hall's Farm to Honorable Ann Veneman Secretary of Agriculture on January 29, 2003 (Letter).

[173] USDA Office of the Secretary National Appeals Division Appeal Determination Case No. 2002S001180 November 7, 2002.

[174] George Hall of Hall's Farm to Honorable Ann Veneman Secretary of Agriculture on January 29, 2003 (Letter).

[175] USDA Office of the Secretary National Appeals Division Appeal Determination Case No. 2002S001180 November 7, 2002.

[176] George Hall of Hall's Farm to National Appeals Division Southern Regional Office on August 15, 2002 (letter).

[177] USDA Office of the Secretary National Appeals Division Appeal Determination Case No. 2002S001180 November 7, 2002.

[178] Matthew 5:43-48

[179] Matthew 7:12

[180] (December 12, 2001.) The Democrat Vol. 110, No. 50. Greene County.

CHAPTER 18

[181] George Hall of Hall's Farm to Honorable Ann Veneman Secretary of Agriculture on January 29, 2003 (Letter).

[182] George Hall of Hall's Farm to National Appeals Division Southern Regional Office on August 15, 2002 (letter).

[183] USDA Office of the Secretary National Appeals Division Appeal Determination Case No. 2002S001180 November 7, 2002.

[184] USDA Office of the Secretary National Appeals Division Appeal Determination Case No. 2002S001180 November 7, 2002.

[185] USDA Office of the Secretary National Appeals Division Appeal Determination Case No. 2002S001180 November 7, 2002.

[186] James E. Currington, USDA Farm Loan Officer to George W. Hall on August 9, 2002 (Letter).

[187] George Hall of Hall's Farm to Honorable Ann Veneman Secretary of Agriculture on January 29, 2003 (Letter).

[188] James E. Currington, USDA Farm Loan Officer to George W. Hall on August 9, 2002 (Letter).

[189] James E. Currington, USDA Farm Loan Officer to George W. Hall on August 9, 2002 (Letter).

[190] USDA Office of the Secretary National Appeals Division Appeal Determination Case No. 2002S001180 November 7, 2002.

[191] USDA Office of the Secretary National Appeals Division Appeal Determination Case No. 2002S001180 November 7, 2002.

[192] USDA Office of the Secretary National Appeals Division Appeal Determination Case No. 2002S001180 November 7, 2002.

[193] USDA Office of the Secretary National Appeals Division Appeal Determination Case No. 2002S001180 November 7, 2002.

[194] George Hall of Hall's Farm to Honorable Ann Veneman Secretary of Agriculture on January 29, 2003 (Letter).

[195] George Hall of Hall's Farm to Honorable Ann Veneman Secretary of Agriculture on January 29, 2003 (Letter).

[196] George Hall of Hall's Farm to Honorable Ann Veneman Secretary of Agriculture on January 29, 2003 (Letter).

[197] George Hall of Hall's Farm to Honorable Ann Veneman Secretary of Agriculture on January 29, 2003 (Letter).

CHAPTER 20

[198] Complaint from George Hall to Office of Bar Counsel Board on Professional Responsibility D.C. Court of Appeals. September 16, 2003.

[199] US District Court Northern District of Alabama Western Division CV-04-CO-0971-W Complaint Breach of Agreement and Retaliation Filed May 12, 2004. From Hall's personal records.

[200] US District Court Northern District of Alabama Western Division CV-04-CO-0971-W Complaint Breach of Agreement and Retaliation Filed May 12, 2004. From Hall's personal records.

[201] US District Court Northern District of Alabama Western Division CV-04-CO-0971-W Complaint Breach of Agreement and Retaliation Filed May 12, 2004. From Hall's personal records.

[202] US District Court Northern District of Alabama Western Division CV-04-CO-0971-W Complaint Breach of Agreement and Retaliation Filed May 12, 2004. From Hall's personal records.

[203] US District Court Northern District of Alabama Western Division CV-04-CO-0971-W Complaint Breach of Agreement and Retaliation Filed May 12, 2004. From Hall's personal records.

[204] US District Court Northern District of Alabama Western Division CV-04-CO-0971-W Complaint Breach of Agreement and Retaliation Filed May 12, 2004. From Hall's personal records.

[205] US District Court Northern District of Alabama Western Division CV-04-CO-0971-W Memorandum of Opinion November 15, 2004 Retrieved from https://www.govinfo.gov/content/pkg/USCOURTS-alnd-7_04-cv-00971/pdf/USCOURTS-alnd-7_04-cv-00971-0.pdf on July 27, 2020.

[206] US District Court Northern District of Alabama Western Division CV-04-CO-0971-W Memorandum of Opinion November 15, 2004 Retrieved from https://www.govinfo.gov/content/pkg/USCOURTS-alnd-7_04-cv-00971/pdf/USCOURTS-alnd-7_04-cv-00971-0.pdf on July 27, 2020.

[207] US District Court Northern District of Alabama Western Division CV-04-CO-0971-W Memorandum of Opinion November 15, 2004 Retrieved from https://www.govinfo.gov/content/pkg/USCOURTS-alnd-7_04-cv-00971/pdf/USCOURTS-alnd-7_04-cv-00971-0.pdf on July 27, 2020.

[208] US District Court Northern District of Alabama Western Division CV-04-CO-0971-W Memorandum of Opinion November 15, 2004 Retrieved from https://www.govinfo.gov/content/pkg/USCOURTS-alnd-7_04-cv-00971/pdf/USCOURTS-alnd-7_04-cv-00971-0.pdf on July 27, 2020.

[209] US District Court Northern District of Alabama Western Division CV-04-CO-0971-W Memorandum of Opinion November 15, 2004

Retrieved from https://www.govinfo.gov/content/pkg/USCOURTS-alnd-7_04-cv-00971/pdf/USCOURTS-alnd-7_04-cv-00971-0.pdf on July 27, 2020.

[210] US District Court Northern District of Alabama Western Division CV-04-CO-0971-W Memorandum of Opinion November 15, 2004 Retrieved from https://www.govinfo.gov/content/pkg/USCOURTS-alnd-7_04-cv-00971/pdf/USCOURTS-alnd-7_04-cv-00971-0.pdf on July 27, 2020.

[211] US District Court Northern District of Alabama Western Division CV-04-CO-0971-W Memorandum of Opinion November 15, 2004 Retrieved from https://www.govinfo.gov/content/pkg/USCOURTS-alnd-7_04-cv-00971/pdf/USCOURTS-alnd-7_04-cv-00971-0.pdf on July 27, 2020.

[212] US District Court Northern District of Alabama Western Division CV-04-CO-0971-W Memorandum of Opinion November 15, 2004 Retrieved from https://www.govinfo.gov/content/pkg/USCOURTS-alnd-7_04-cv-00971/pdf/USCOURTS-alnd-7_04-cv-00971-0.pdf on July 27, 2020.

[213] US District Court Northern District of Alabama Western Division CV-04-CO-0971-W Memorandum of Opinion November 15, 2004 Retrieved from https://www.govinfo.gov/content/pkg/USCOURTS-alnd-7_04-cv-00971/pdf/USCOURTS-alnd-7_04-cv-00971-0.pdf on July 27, 2020.

[214] Memorandum of Opinion United States District Court Northern District of Alabama Western Division Case CV-04-CO-0971-W January 31, 2006, Retrieved from https://www.govinfo.gov/content/pkg/USCOURTS-alnd-7_04-cv-00971/pdf/USCOURTS-alnd-7_04-cv-00971-1.pdf on July 27, 2020.

[215] Memorandum of Opinion United States District Court Northern District of Alabama Western Division Case CV-04-CO-0971-W January 31, 2006, Retrieved from https://www.govinfo.gov/content/pkg/USCOURTS-alnd-7_04-cv-00971/pdf/USCOURTS-alnd-7_04-cv-00971-1.pdf on July 27, 2020.

[216] Memorandum of Opinion United States District Court Northern District of Alabama Western Division Case CV-04-CO-0971-W January 31, 2006, Retrieved from https://www.govinfo.gov/content/pkg/USCOURTS-alnd-7_04-cv-00971/pdf/USCOURTS-alnd-7_04-cv-00971-1.pdf on July 27, 2020.

[217] USDA Office of the Secretary National Appeals Division Appeal Determination Case No. 2002S001180 November 7, 2002.

[218] Memorandum of Opinion United States District Court Northern District of Alabama Western Division Case CV-04-CO-0971-W January 31, 2006, Retrieved from https://www.govinfo.gov/content/pkg/USCOURTS-alnd-7_04-cv-00971/pdf/USCOURTS-alnd-7_04-cv-00971-1.pdf on July 27, 2020.

[219] Memorandum of Opinion United States District Court Northern District of Alabama Western Division Case CV-04-CO-0971-W January 31, 2006, Retrieved from https://www.govinfo.gov/content/pkg/USCOURTS-alnd-7_04-cv-00971/pdf/USCOURTS-alnd-7_04-cv-00971-1.pdf on July 27, 2020.

[220] Memorandum of Opinion United States District Court Northern District of Alabama Western Division Case CV-04-CO-0971-W January 31, 2006, Retrieved from https://www.govinfo.gov/content/pkg/USCOURTS-alnd-7_04-cv-00971/pdf/USCOURTS-alnd-7_04-cv-00971-1.pdf on July 27, 2020.

[221] US Court of Federal Claims No. 05-517C Hall v the United States October 31, 2005 Retrieved from https://cite.case.law/fed-cl/69/51/ on July 27, 2020.

[222] US Court of Federal Claims No. 05-517C Hall v the United States October 31, 2005 Retrieved from https://cite.case.law/fed-cl/69/51/ on July 27, 2020.

[223] Memorandum Opinion and Order United States Court of Federal Claims No. 05-517C Filed October 31, 2005. Retrieved from https://casetext.com/case/hall-v-us-49 on July 27, 2020.

[224] Memorandum Opinion and Order United States Court of Federal Claims No. 05-517C Filed October 31, 2005. Retrieved from https://casetext.com/case/hall-v-us-49 on July 27, 2020.

[225] US Court of Federal Claims No. 05-517C Hall v the United States October 31, 2005 Retrieved from https://cite.case.law/fed-cl/69/51/ on July 27, 2020.

[226] US Court of Federal Claims No. 05-517C Hall v the United States October 31, 2005 Retrieved from https://cite.case.law/fed-cl/69/51/ on July 27, 2020.

[227] US Court of Federal Claims No. 05-517C Hall v the United States October 31, 2005 Retrieved from https://cite.case.law/fed-cl/69/51/ on July 27, 2020.

[228] Memorandum Opinion and Order United States Court of Federal Claims No. 05-517C Filed October 31, 2005. Retrieved from https://casetext.com/case/hall-v-us-49 on July 27, 2020.

[229] Memorandum Opinion and Order United States Court of Federal Claims No. 05-517C Filed October 31, 2005. Retrieved from https://casetext.com/case/hall-v-us-49 on July 27, 2020.

[230] Unpublished Opinion by U.S. Court of Appeals for the Eleventh Circuit on November 29, 2006 on Appeal from the U.S. District Court for the Northern District of Alabama, No. 06-11431 D.C. Docket No. 04-00971-CV-CO-W retrieved from http://media.ca11.uscourts.gov/opinions/unpub/files/200611431.pdf on July 28, 2020

[231] Petition for Rehearing En Banc US Court of Appeals for the Eleventh Circuit No. 06-11431-DD January 16, 2007 from Author's Collection.

[232] Petition for Rehearing En Banc US Court of Appeals for the Eleventh Circuit No. 06-11431-DD January 16, 2007 from Author's Collection.

[233] Petition for Rehearing En Banc US Court of Appeals for the Eleventh Circuit No. 06-11431-DD January 16, 2007 from Author's Collection.

[234] Petition for Rehearing En Banc US Court of Appeals for the Eleventh Circuit No. 06-11431-DD January 16, 2007 from Author's Collection.

[235] Petition for Rehearing En Banc US Court of Appeals for the Eleventh Circuit No. 06-11431-DD January 16, 2007 from Author's Collection.

[236] Petition for Rehearing En Banc US Court of Appeals for the Eleventh Circuit No. 06-11431-DD January 16, 2007 from Author's Collection.

[237] Petition for Rehearing En Banc US Court of Appeals for the Eleventh Circuit No. 06-11431-DD January 16, 2007 from Author's Collection.

[238] Petition for Rehearing En Banc US Court of Appeals for the Eleventh Circuit No. 06-11431-DD January 16, 2007 from Author's Collection.

[239] Petition for Rehearing En Banc US Court of Appeals for the Eleventh Circuit No. 06-11431-DD January 16, 2007 from Author's Collection.

[240] Petition for Rehearing En Banc US Court of Appeals for the Eleventh Circuit No. 06-11431-DD January 16, 2007 from Author's Collection.

[241] Hall v. Johanns; 240 Fed. Appx. 407, 11th Cir. (Ala.), Mar. 02, 2007.

[242] US Court of Federal Claims No. 05-517C Settlement Agreement March 28, 2007 from Author's Collection.

[243] US Court of Federal Claims No. 05-517C Settlement Agreement March 28, 2007 from Author's Collection.

[244] US Court of Federal Claims No. 05-517C Settlement Agreement March 28, 2007 from Author's Collection.

[245] US Court of Federal Claims No. 05-517C Settlement Agreement March 28, 2007 from Author's Collection.

[246] US Court of Federal Claims No. 05-517C Settlement Agreement March 28, 2007 from Author's Collection.

[247] Cornell Law School Legal Information Institute Retrieved from https://www.law.cornell.edu/uscode/text/7/1991 on July 29, 2020.

[248] Cornell Law School Legal Information Institute Retrieved from https://www.law.cornell.edu/uscode/text/7/2008h on July 29, 2020.

[249] Cornell Law School Legal Information Institute Retrieved from https://www.law.cornell.edu/uscode/text/7/1991 on July 29, 2020.

CHAPTER 22

[250] USDA Certificate of Election to George W. Hall for 3 year term on Greene/Sumter County FSA Committee January 1, 2008. Author's records.

[251] Certificate of Retirement from the Armed Forces of the USA to Master Sergeant (E8) George W. Hall on February 22, 2008. Author's records.

[252] University of Alabama Rural Medical Scholars Program to George Hall for Outstanding Community Partner in Alabama Agromedicine. (Award) Author's records.

[253] (July 27, 2014.) "Greene County Marks 45th Year Since Historic Election." *Tuscaloosa News*. Retrieved on April 11, 2020 from https://www.tuscaloosanews.com/news/20140727/greene-county-marks-45th-year-since-historic-election

[254] (July 27, 2014.) "Greene County Marks 45th Year Since Historic Election." *Tuscaloosa News*. Retrieved on April 11, 2020 from https://www.tuscaloosanews.com/news/20140727/greene-county-marks-45th-year-since-historic-election

[255] (July 27, 2014.) "Greene County Marks 45th Year Since Historic Election." *Tuscaloosa News*. Retrieved on April 11, 2020 from https://www.tuscaloosanews.com/news/20140727/greene-county-marks-45th-year-since-historic-election